Contemporary Spanish Fiction

Contemporary Spanish Fiction

Generation X

Dorothy Odartey-Wellington

Newark: University of Delaware Press

Associated University Presses
2010 Eastpark Boulevard
Cranbury, NJ 08512

The paper used in this publication meets the requirements of the American National Standard for Permanence of Paper for Printed Library Materials Z39.48-1984.

Library of Congress Cataloging-in-Publication Data

Odartey-Wellington, Dorothy, 1964–
    Contemporary Spanish fiction : Generation X / Dorothy Odartey-Wellington.
        p.   cm.
    Includes bibliographical references and index.
    ISBN 978-0-87413-008-9 (alk. paper)
    1. Spanish fiction—20th century—History and criticism.   I. Title.
    PQ6144.O33   2008
    863'.6409—dc22   2007038321

In Memoriam
Sebastian Suárez Barrios
(1978–2007)

Contents

7

Acknowledgments

I WOULD LIKE TO RECOGNIZE THE MINISTERIO DE ASUNTOS EXTERIores y de Cooperación—Agencia Española de Cooperación Internacional (Spain) and the College of Arts, University of Guelph (Canada) for the grants that made it possible for me to carry out research for this book.

I am grateful to the following authors and their publishers for permission to quote excerpts from their novels: Belén Gopegui, and Editorial Anagrama for *La conquista del aire,* 1998; José Ángel Mañas and Ediciones Destino, S.A. for *Historias del Kronen,* 1994; Antonio Orejudo Utrilla, Lengua de Trapo, and Tusquets Editores for *Fabulosas narraciones por historias,* 1996; Antonio Orejudo Utrilla and Grupo Santillana de Ediciones for *Ventajas de viajar en tren,* 2000.

Many thanks also to the editors of *Confluencia* and *Revista Hispánica Moderna* for granting me permission to publish in this book versions of my articles "De Madrid al cielo: Una novela de la Generación X española inspirada en el cine negro," *Confluencia* 20.1 (2004): 63–71 and "La tecnología, el espacio urbano y el sujeto en la narrativa joven española," *Revista Hispánica Moderna* 55.1 (2002): 204–10.

A special thank you to my colleague Norman Cheadle, Laurentian University (Canada), for agreeing to read the final draft of the manuscript.

Contemporary
Spanish Fiction

Introduction

"GENERACIÓN X," "GENERACIÓN KRONEN," "PRIMERA GENERACIÓN
de escritores de la democracia española," and "Narradores españoles novísimos de los años noventa" are a few of the designa-
tions that have been used to describe Spanish novelists who were
born between 1960 and 1970 and who published their first novels
in the last decade of the twentieth century.[1] Spanish Generation
X novelists are motivated by a concern with identity formation and
self-assertion in a changing economic, technological, and sociopolitical landscape. They write within a transnational context and lo-
cate their subjects and their narratives in the so-called free market
economy, the consumer culture, and the media environment in
order to call into question their subjects' autonomy in the identity-
forming process of postmodernity. In this contemporary milieu
they cast doubt on the myths of autonomy or freedom and on similar assumptions related to the realities of postcapitalist societies.

Unlike their "movida" predecessors, for example, the characters
in Spanish Generation X novels do not find any justification for
celebrating the plastic, unpredictable, and incoherent postmodern
subject or the myth of postmodern freeplay and autonomy within
an increasingly unstable sociopolitical and economic world. Critic
Cristina Moreiras Menor has observed that in contrast to the
1980s subject who reveled in its plasticity and immersed itself in
postmodernity as a means of disassociating himself/herself from
"its recent past of [shared] repression, silence and homogeneity,"
the 1990s subject wakes up to the horrors of the "logics of the
society of spectacle" in which he or she had previously found "important spaces for the construction and representation of identities" (2000, 136). This questioning of the subject's ability to attain
autonomy and affirm its identity in the media-dominated, market-
driven environment is one of the common threads that link this
seemingly diverse group of writers in Spain.

The Generation X writers' preoccupation with identities that

13

are weakened rather than affirmed in the media-dominated, market-driven globalized environment is evident in the recurrent image of solitary and alienated characters in their novels. Within this environment their characters appear to be caught in an overrepresented present that is detached from the past. As a consequence, their sense of self is further destabilized since identity and agency tend to be rooted in history.

Indeed, by engaging with identity and agency in the current globalized socioeconomic and political milieu, these Spanish novelists deal with realities beyond the narrow geographical space that they share with one another. The themes with which they are concerned are of a transnational, rather than national, nature and they correspond to circumstances that affect today's postindustrial society as a whole.

In exploring the impact of media and market explosion on agency, Spanish Generation X novelists straddle the divide between high and low culture. Consequently they have sometimes been dismissed by some critics as being driven by the market to regurgitate products of American popular culture that they supposedly consume massively in the first place. Such a view is a misreading of Spanish Generation X novelists. They do not merely mimic the contemporary American-dominated culture but rather challenge its attempt to control their subjects' autonomy.

Spanish Generation X novelists' engagement with the identity of their subjects within what they perceive to be a debilitating socioeconomic and cultural context is accompanied by a concern with the impact of the same environment on themselves as authors. They deal with their own sense of vulnerability as authors within an environment in which the lines between reality and fiction, history and representation, as well as literature and commodity are blurred. Many of them express their feeling of dislocation in this context through a metafictional approach to writing in which they question the security implied in the notion of author.

In the past decade, a few critics have attempted a description of Spanish Generation X fictions according to their recurrent themes, their narrative structure, and their language, as well as the sociocultural contexts that influence their creation. The leading Generation X apologist to date is Germán Gullón who dismisses the apocalyptic notion that the relatively young novelists are just products of a destructive television and video culture passing off their indolence and nihilistic worldview as literature. Commenting on the crude reality that forms the main substance of some Generation X novels and is a source of aggravation for some critics, Gullón concedes that "su fuerte no reside en la prosapia estética" (their strength is not based on illustrious aesthetics) (1996, 31). In his opinion the novels in question have redeeming qualities that are unlikely to be appreciated by traditional methods of criticism based solely on indicators of aesthetic and sociopolitical engagement. Gullón points to the inability or refusal of some critical sensibilities to adjust to a changing cultural climate:

Cansa ya leer a trasnochados peroratistas quejarse de si la televisión y el vídeo destruyen la cultura. Lo que ocurre es bien sencillo: nunca antes en la historia de la humanidad el creador había disfrutado de tantísimas opciones, en todos los ámbitos, desde la libertad para representar hábitos personales . . . hasta la capacidad de formalizar sus representaciones en una miríada de opciones. (ibid.)

[It is tiresome to read obsolete complaints that television and video are destroying culture. What is happening is quite simple: never before in the history of humanity has the creator enjoyed so many options in all spheres; from the freedom to represent personal habits . . . to the ability to formalize his/her representations in a myriad of options.]

Gullón's observations highlight two important facts that should not be overlooked. Subject matter in fiction is no longer confined to issues in the public sphere; more importantly, the medium of communication has expanded beyond the boundaries of the printed form to embrace other modes of expression commonly associated with popular entertainment. Apart from drawing attention to the diversity in communication modes and vital issues, Gullón suggests that critics take into consideration the changing modes of production and distribution. He urges that:

Para comprenderlos y evaluarlos debemos aceptar, pues, el impacto que en el escritor actual tiene la sociedad y los medios de comunicación, es decir, que la autoría conlleva hoy un mayor porcentaje de influencia social . . . Hoy los libros se componen y editan, paradójicamente, con menor libertad por parte del artista, porque los editores, la comercialización y demás los afecta quizá en exceso. (ibid.)

[In order to understand and evaluate them, we must acknowledge the impact that society and the communication media have on the contemporary writer; that is, authorship today entails a greater degree of social influence . . . Today books are written and published, paradoxically, with less freedom on the part of the writer because publishers, marketing, etcetera, affect them, perhaps excessively.]

Toni Dorca has also observed that there is a tendency to dismiss many of the young writers as merely exploiting, under the guise of subversion, "las ansias de consumo de la sociedad" (society's longings for consumption) (1997, 310). Indeed, unlike Gullón, Toni Dorca is not quick to dismiss these allegations entirely. Rather, he wonders:

¿[T]enemos derecho críticos y profesores a censurar a los jóvenes por acercar la literatura al público y venderse al mejor postor?; dicho en otras palabras, ¿es lícito censurar que una porción cada vez mayor de jóvenes sin empleo se procure un sustento mediante la escritura? (ibid., 311)

[Do we, professors and critics, have the right to censure young writers for narrowing the gap between the public and literature and for selling themselves to the highest bidder? In other words, is it acceptable to criticize the fact that an increasing number of unemployed young people are trying to earn a living through writing?]

He, too, decries the partisan nature of existing criticism and suggests "un sistema axiológico que sustituya las nociones estéticas de antaño" (an axiological system that replaces old aesthetic notions) (ibid.). In other words, he calls for the contextualization of these novels to enable their effective analysis.

For her part Carmen de Urioste situates the new narrative in a specific socioeconomic context that determines its very nature. She describes this context as follows:

[L]a cultura española . . . de consumo, basada en las industrias culturales y de la comunicación, en los *mass media,* en la publicidad y en los espectáculos . . . [E]s decir, una cultura que avanza desde una definición elitista y restringida de la misma hacia la incorporación dentro de ella de los avances tecnológicos y de la cultura de masas o comercial (programas de televisión, música, literatura popular, moda, cine, video). (1997, 456)

[The Spanish . . . consumer culture, based on the cultural and communication industries, the mass media, advertising, and spectacle . . .
That is, a culture that moves from an elitist and restricted definition of
itself toward the incorporation of technological advancements and
mass or commercial culture (television programs, music, popular literature, fashion, cinema, video).]

By this statement Urioste is placing Generation X narratives right
within the "cultural logic of late capitalism" in which the very
boundaries of commodity have expanded into the spaces hitherto
reserved for high culture (Jameson, 1991, 2). To disregard cultural
expressions deemed to be commodities is to ignore the insights
that they offer into the very period that engendered them.

The three critics mentioned above call for the need to ground
the present Generation X narratives in a specific historical, social,
cultural, and even economic context. In the main, they allude to
the fact that to arrive at a sound analysis of these works, critics
must be conscious of the fact that the very foundations of creative
expression and its distribution have undergone extensive transformation in the last century. They all suggest that we are dealing
with a whole new phenomenon that invalidates traditional criteria
of evaluation.

To date, this group of novelists has been the focus of at least one
anthology (*Páginas amarillas*, 1997), a collection of interviews
(*¿Qué he hecho yo para publicar esto?: XX escritores jóvenes para
el siglo XXI*, 1999), and debates in several media, as well as articles in scholarly journals outlining their characteristics. In a recent
book that brings together sociology and literary analysis, *Sociología de valores en la novela española contemporánea/La generación X* (2003), Antonio Gutiérrez Resa draws on the novels of
some of these writers to examine the nature of contemporary
Spanish values. In addition, some representative members of the
group have been the recipients of important literary prizes in
Spanish fiction in the last few years. Yet the question still remains
as to whether the 1990s produced a literary generation at all. For
some the so-called Generation X group of Spanish writers is a
media invention, and to others this generation is a mere sociological phenomenon not unlike the hippie and yuppie generations of
the sixties and eighties, respectively.

This newest generation faces the challenge for recognition in

part because of the heterogeneity of the literary environment in
Spain in the 1990s. In Santos Alonso's review of Spanish fiction
between 1975 and 2001, he identifies the existence of at least six
active generations in the last few decades of the previous century.
The generation that was lauded for the revival of Spanish narrative
in the context of sterile and univocal narratives inspired by the official version of the civil war was still present on the literary scene
in the 1990s. Camilo José Cela (1915–2002), for example, won the
Nobel Prize for Literature in 1989 and the prestigious Premio Cervantes in 1995 after winning the Planeta in 1994 for *La cruz de
San Andrés;* Miguel Delibes (1920) won the Premio Cervantes in
1993 and the Premio Nacional de Narrativa in 1999; Torrente Bal-
lester (1910–99) received the Premio Azorín for fiction in 1994
and continued to publish in the last decade before his death in
1999. Among the generation of the so-called "niños de la guerra"
(also known as the "generación de medio siglo"), renowned for
their social realist novels of the fifties and the experimental fiction
of the sixties, Carmen Martín Gaite (1925–2000), Juan Marsé
(1933–   ), and Ana María Matute (1926–   ) continued to add
their voices to the ongoing themes in narrative fiction. Marsé
wrote of the recuperation of memory in *Rabos de Lagartija;* Matute elicited discussion on fantastic fiction with *El olvidado rey de
Gudu;* and on the subject of fiction itself as its own theme, Martín
Gaite wrote *La reina de las nieves.* The next generation, who
Alonso describes as having lived and written in the shadow of the
previous one, has a provocative, prolific, and critically visible representative in the person of Francisco Umbral, whose status in
contemporary Spanish fictions is attested to by his winning such
prestigious prizes as the Cervantes (2000), the Nacional de Letras
Españolas (1997), and the Príncipe de Asturias (1996). Currently
the literary scene is dominated by writers of the "Generación del
75" and those of the "Generación de los 80" who have earned
their place as established writers. Álvaro Pombo (1939), of the
Generación del 75, is considered to be one of the greatest novelists
of contemporary Spanish fiction, and he has recently been elected
to the Real Academia Española. Of the latter generation, perhaps
Antonio Muñoz Molina is one of the best known and one of the
most successful.

Given this illustrious and heterogeneous list of contemporaneous Spanish writers in 1990s Spain, one can appreciate the diffi-

culty of identifying a role model or a set of role models for the youngest generation. Furthermore, the latter is faced with the challenge of attaining canonicity in an already saturated environment of several already established writers.

In addition, the heterogeneity of the Generation X group of writers itself gets in the way of its categorization. Antonio Orejudo Utrilla, a member of the generation, notes this when he writes that

> Además, a la hora de caracterizar la literatura de la época democrática, y especialmente la narrativa de la última generación, todos ellos [críticos] coinciden en señalar que su principal característica es precisamente la ausencia de características comunes, la inexistencia de una tendencia dominante. ¿Qué tiene en común Lorenzo Silva con Lucía Etxebarria, Luis Magrinyà con José Ángel Mañas, Martínez de Pisón con Andrés Ibáñez, ambos con Ángela Vallvey, y todos ellos con Belén Gopegui? (2004, 7)

> [Furthermore, when it comes to characterizing the literature of the democratic period, and especially the narrative of the most recent generation, they [critics] all point out that their main distinguishing feature is their lack of common characteristics or any dominant tendency. What has Lorenzo Silva got in common with Lucía Etxebarria, Luis Magrinyà with José Ángel Mañas, Martínez de Pisón with Andrés Ibáñez, both with Ángela Vallvey, and all of them with Belén Gopegui?]

Orejudo Utrilla rightly observes that these young writers, who had not experienced Francoism to the full, unlike the previous generation, and who really came of age in the period of democracy, are not driven by a desire to rebel against paradigms. As such they are not united around, or identified by, a common goal:

> [L]a última generación del siglo XX (o la primera del siglo XXI) carece de un padre literario, de una tradición en contra de la cual pueda afirmarse. Esta generación sale a la palestra literaria en un tiempo en cierto modo virgen: no hay, como en otras épocas, una corriente dominante. (ibid.)

> [The last generation of the 20th century (or the first of the 21st century) does not have a literary father, a tradition against which they can assert themselves. This generation comes onto the literary scene at a time that, in a certain way, is completely untried: unlike in other periods, there isn't a dominant trend.]

The absence of *obvious* unifying tendencies in this generation is underscored by a drive toward individuality in a saturated cultural marketplace:

> Los escritores de esta generación no creen en la elaboración de proyectos comunes, sino en la propia salvación a través del talento individual. Nunca ha habido tanta actividad literaria y ha sido al mismo tiempo tan difícil hablar de una generación literaria. Quienes supuestamente deberían formar parte de ella parecen huir con su comportamiento y, sobre todo, con su literatura de cualquier intento de sistematización y agrupamiento. (ibid., 7–8)

> [The writers of this generation do not believe in the creation of common projects, but rather in their own personal salvation through individual talent. There has never been so much literary activity and yet so little possibility of speaking of a literary generation. Those who, supposedly, should form part of it appear to flee with their behavior and, especially, with their literature, from any attempt at systematization and association.]

In addition to the heterogeneity of the group, as identified by Orejudo Utrilla, the classification of Spanish Generation X fiction is further challenged by its location in a global rather than a limited national framework. The panorama of contemporary Spanish fiction is expanded, according to Gonzalo Navajas, by its postnational frame of reference. He explains that unlike in the Francoist period when literary practices were predicated upon by national cultural, literary, social and political concerns, narrative fiction today, like contemporary Spanish cinema, is inscribed in and forms "parte integral del paradigma global de la cultura" (an integral part of the global paradigm of culture) (2004, 13). Citing film directors Pedro Almodóvar, Alejandro Amenábar, and Icíar Bollaín as examples, he observes that their work "se parte de un núcleo referencial inmediato y reconocible . . . pero el tratamiento de ese núcleo temático se hace empleando un lenguaje y procedimientos que van dirigidos a un destinatario que trasciende el entorno estrictamente nacional" (sets out from an immediate and recognizable point of reference . . . but the treatment of that thematic nucleus is done using a language and methods that are directed toward an addressee that transcends the strictly national context) (ibid.). He concludes that

Escribir novela hoy—la mejor novela, la que genera una discursividad narrativa diferencial y no es meramente una reproducción formulaica de lo existente—es hacerlo para el mundo y para un lector ideal colectivo que condensa los parámetros de la cultura contemporánea. (ibid., 14)

[To write a novel today—the best novel, the kind that is generated by a differential narrative discursiveness and is not merely a formulaic reproduction of existing models—is to write it for an ideal collective world or readership that represents contemporary culture.]

Within these international cultural parameters, in his opinion, the components of contemporary Spanish cultural production cannot be expected to be conventional and canonical (ibid., 13). It is within this vibrant, active and amorphous literary environment that the newest generation in the last decade of the twentieth century attempts to make way for itself. Such a varied literary environment, in which writers of different stripes, backgrounds, histories, influences, and motivations converge in one period, affords one the opportunity to consider the limitations of canonicity and explore the fictionalizing nature of the processes of granting acceptance to some authors.

Finally, critics' acceptance of this new generation has been hampered by what has been seen as a media and market strategy to promote youth as the defining characteristic of the Generation X group of writers. Indeed, the 1990s saw the largest output of publications by "young" writers than any other period in Spanish literary history.[2] To some critics the sign that the boom of youth writing was definitely out of control came when, in 1996, a fourteen-year-old girl, Violeta Hernando, published her first novel.[3] The editor of *Páginas amarillas*, the first anthology of works by the young generation of the 1990s, Sabas Martín, attributes the phenomenon of the explosion of novels by "young" writers to the critical success of José Ángel Mañas's *Historias del Kronen*, which was published when Mañas was only twenty-four years old.

Although the coincidence of youth and literary success is rare, it is not unknown in Spanish literary history.[4] However, it seemed that in the 1990s the young age of a novelist was not incidental to his or her output. Youth appeared to have become in itself an element of literary value. Prestigious publishers such as Anagrama, Planeta, and Plaza y Janés published and promoted the works of then first-time novelists like Ismael Grasa, Belén Gopegui, Eloy Tizón, and Ray Loriga. They went even further to endorse these new novelists' works by awarding them some of their most sought-after literary prizes. In the past decade some of the most prestigious prizes have gone to then-young and new names like Lucía Etxebarria who won Destino's Nadal in 1998 for *Beatriz y los cuerpos celestes.* In 1996 the Nadal went to Pedro Maestre, for *Matando dinosaurios con tirachinas.* Lorenzo Silva won it in 2000 with *El alquimista impaciente.* Planeta's Premio Planeta went to Juan Manuel de Prada in 1997 for *La tempestad.* In 1999, Espido Freire became the youngest winner of the Planeta with *Melocotones helados.*

Newer literary prizes were also created with a vision to recognizing new talents. Hence the younger writers found exposure through the publishing house Lengua de Trapo, for example, which was established in 1995. However, in reaction to what they saw as a trend in promoting youth, Lengua de Trapo insisted on innovation. In the Spanish newspaper *El País*, it was announced at the time that "Lengua de Trapo es una editorial que nace con la intención de dar cabida a las nuevas generaciones de escritores. Más que la edad o el sexo, los responsables de la editorial aseguran que buscan una nueva mirada narrativa" (Lengua de Trapo was founded to make room for the newer generations of writers. The people in charge of the publishing house affirm that they are motivated by a search for new narrative styles rather than by age or gender).[5]

The abundance of publications by young and previously unheard-of writers raised the suspicion of critics and already established writers. They saw the publishing houses as focusing on youth for commercial purposes. While some proclaimed the birth of a new generation of novelists, others cried foul, alleging that the so-called new generation was a false one. They saw it as an invention born out of the interested conspiracy among publishers, literary agents, and the media, who were thriving in an environment given more to the dictates of the market than to promoting literary excellence. This opinion is no doubt shared by Ramón Acín who poses the rhetorical question:

> ¿A qué responde ese interés actual en torno a lo "joven" como motivo publicitario y de esperanza—algo apenas cubierto desde el comienzo

de los 80—dada la nombradía, comercial o literaria y aunque sea
parcelada, de autores jóvenes como Loriga o Mañas entre otros?
(1996, 6)

[Why this current interest in "youth" as a reason for publicity and
hope—something that has hardly been a secret since the beginning of
the eighties—given the literary or commercial fame, albeit selective, of
young authors like Loriga or Mañas among others?]

He echoes similar misgivings about the state of Spanish literature in observations published in the culture section of newspapers such as *El País*. Some of the headlines in *El País* in the 1990s
summarize the concerns that critics and writers had about the
quality of literary production and the cultural climate in general
during that decade: "El mercado impone una literatura ligera"
(The market is creating a light literature); "La literatura supeditada a las leyes del mercado" (Literature dependent on the laws of
the market); "La literatura se volvió mercado pero hay que tener
fe en las letras" (Literature has become commercialized but one
has to have faith in the Arts).[6]

Indeed the very factors that challenge the identification of the
Generation X novelists in Spain are symptomatic of the cultural
and socioeconomic environment that has led to the birth of these
writers with a particular way of viewing and reflecting the world
in which they operate. To proceed then beyond the partisan or
apologetic approach to the Generation X writers and to enable
their works to stand on their own as autonomous creations with
their own logic, there is the need to heed Walter Benjamin's statement that "[d]uring long periods of history, the mode of human
sense perception changes together with humanity's entire mode of
existence. The manner in which human sense perception is orga-
nized and the medium through which it is accomplished, is determined not only by nature but by historical circumstances as well"
(quoted in Hall 1998, 505). Therefore, I will be examining Spanish
Generation X fiction within the context of the contemporary period described variously as postindustrial, postcapitalist, consumer, global, media, or information society. This is the context
that has determined the content and the mode of expression of
Spanish Generation X fiction.

My analysis also takes into account the heterogeneity of the

works in question. The variety of vital contexts that inspire Spanish Generation X fiction, the vast array of influences, both popular
and literary, on their writing, and their varying perspectives with
regard to the identified common themes that motivate their writing make of this group of Spanish writers an atomized or a fragmented entity. Furthermore, the very nature of the circumstances
to which they are opposed obliges them to so individualize their
subjects and their perspectives that they undermine any possibility
of being viewed as engaged in a common project of dissent. I have
therefore selected the novels for this study to reflect the heterogeneity and multiplicity of perspectives that characterize Spanish
Generation X fictions. In this book, the newest generation of
Spanish novelists are represented by the sociopolitically conscious
writers Ismael Grasa (*De Madrid al cielo* [1994] [Madrid, the
Next Best Thing to Heaven]) and Belén Gopegui (*La conquista
del aire* [1998] [The Conquest of Air] and *Lo real* [2001] [The
Real Thing]); their audiovisual, media-oriented contemporaries,
José Ángel Mañas (*Historias del Kronen*) [1994] [Stories from the
Kronen]), Ray Loriga (*La pistola de mi hermano* [1995] [*My
Brother's Gun*]);[7] and Gabriela Bustelo (*Veo veo* [1996] [I spy]);
and the perspicacious critic of the generation, Antonio Orejudo
Utrilla (*Fabulosas narraciones por historias* [1996] [Fantastic
Narratives Passed Off as True Stories] and *Ventajas de viajar en
tren* [2000] [Advantages of Traveling by Train]).

Ray Loriga's *La pistola de mi hermano* has been likened to a
road movie. Its central character is a young disaffected male whose
motives for committing a string of seemingly meaningless murders
during his flight from the law are made even more obscure in their
portrayal through the inadequate medium of television talk shows.
Mañas's *Historias del Kronen* chronicles the summer activities of
several suburban youths who spend most of their time in bars and
are trapped in a cesspool of drugs, sex, and senseless violence.
These two novels, considered to be emblematic of Spanish Generation X fiction, are positioned within the novelistic world of the
North American rock and punk subculture.

Middle-class youth angst and popular video culture, however,
are not the only face of Spanish Generation X fiction. Ismael
Grasa locates *De Madrid al cielo* within a well-established popular
tradition, the detective story. Furthermore, Grasa's characters are
not middle-class urban youths as Generation X characters tend to

be. *De Madrid al cielo* is set in Madrid and the first-person narrator's experiences in the city serve as a pretext for social criticism as well as a reflection on the existential problems of the narrator, a postcapitalist flaneur. Unlike his nineteenth-century counterpart, however, Zenón, the narrator, does not roam the city leisurely for pleasure. His daily walks are acts of survival, as he has to earn a living. Although he and the other characters are not immediately identifiable with the youths of *Historias del Kronen* or *La pistola de mi hermano*, it is clear that they share the same sense of emptiness and alienation from their world.

Extreme alienation is also the predominant theme in Bustelo's *Veo veo*. The first-person twenty-something-year-old narrator's sense of alienation from her surroundings and from others is manifested in her inability to forge profound and lasting relationships with the people she meets in her daily prowls in bars and nightclubs. It is also evident in her constant use of drugs as well as in her obsession with the idea that she is constantly under surveillance.

Belén Gopegui appears to be the most different from all the other novelists. Her novels, *La conquista del aire* and *Lo real,* do not at all reflect the urban problems of drugs, sex, and violence that are often associated with Generation X fictions. She does, however, focus on the generational theme of essential instability and insecurity in the new urban order. In *La conquista del aire,* a rather prosaic event, a young man borrowing money from long-time friends to keep his struggling electronic business afloat, causes all involved to begin to question certain foundations upon which their sense of being is built. Similarly in *Lo real* the vicissitudes of a young professional in the ultra-modern context of media communications enable Gopegui to delve into what she calls "los mecanismos que empañan la hipotética libertad del sujeto" (the mechanisms that tarnish the hypothetical freedom of the subject) (1999, 89). Through these novels she explores the impact of the market environment in which we all live today on the agency of individuals.

Antonio Orejudo Utrilla turns a reflexive eye on his generation in his novels *Ventajas de viajar en tren* and *Fabulosas narraciones por historias*. In *Ventajas de viajar en tren,* Orejudo Utrilla echoes the prevailing theme of alienation in a short novel that revolves around a schizophrenic distortion of reality. Nothing is certain, not even the identity of the multiple narrative voices that could all be the same person or different fictitious people within the fiction. In this novel, Helga Pato, a woman on her way back to Madrid after committing her husband to a psychiatric institution in the north of Spain, is engaged in conversation by a man who claims to be a psychiatrist from that institution. The latter, who calls himself Dr. Sanagustín, leaves behind a red folder containing the stories of patients from the institution when he gets off the train to buy some lunch. When Helga tries to return the folder, she discovers that the man she had met is an imposter who had used the name of his brother-in-law. This turn of events throws into question the authenticity of all the stories that the man had told her on the train.

Orejudo Utrilla's first novel, *Fabulosas narraciones por historias*, is also written in the same metafictional vein. This novel, set mainly in the 1920s, is made up of excerpts of a variety of texts such as fiction, essays, correspondence, pornography, and news items. These are all linked by a central plot—the attempts of a young writer, Patricio Cordero, to publish his first novel. In the Cervantine mode, Orejudo Utrilla turns his vision in his two novels onto the narratives of his time. He examines the publishing conventions, the reading practices, and the marketing strategies, as well as theories of image, identity, and representation in contemporary fiction.

My examination of Orejudo Utrilla's novels serves as an appropriate last chapter to this book. In it I examine Orejudo Utrilla's metafictional mode of writing, which turns a critical focus on the notion of author as representation similar to representations in popular and entertainment culture. In the first chapter, I analyze the two novels that were considered to be representative of Generation X fiction in the 1990s because of their focus on contemporary youth and their values. I show, however, that *Historias del Kronen* and *La pistola de mi hermano* bring out the tensions between the new generation and the section of society that they represented in the 1990s on one hand and the values of the media-oriented, consumer society on the other. These novelists, I argue, are not mere products of audiovisual commodity culture. They are writers engaged with the interaction of textual and audiovisual modes of expression and the impact of the hegemony of the latter and its commercial culture on identity and human relations. The second chapter focuses on *Veo veo* and *De Madrid al cielo,* two novels that are structured on a popular genre, detective fiction. Grasa's and Bustelo's novels provide an appropriate context for portraying urban subjects' ontological uncertainties in a postcapitalist, media-dominated environment. I examine their use of the popular cinematographic genre to reveal their subjects' disconnectedness from the urban setting in the neoliberal, socioeconomic order (Grasa) and in the information technology explosion (Bustelo) associated with the 1990s. The third chapter examines the true nature of so-called democracy in the postcapitalist context of Gopegui's *Lo real* and *La conquista del aire.* It shows that Gopegui takes on the recurrent generational theme of diminished subjects in 1990s Spain through her engagement with the representational nature of democracy and the impact that the combined powers of the market and the media have on agency.

My analysis of these novels will show that all these novelists demonstrate a keen awareness of their subjects' location at the intersection of conflicting social, political, economic and communicative practices, where security and stability of self are threatened rather than affirmed. This point needs to be made to refute the often repeated criticism that these young writers, sometimes dismissed as apathetic products of media and consumer culture, do no more than reproduce what they passively consume. My analysis will also show that Spanish generation X fiction of the 1990s ought to be considered in an international context; that international context, it should be borne in mind, is characterized by globalized economic, social, and cultural practices that are, in general, dominated by the economic and cultural logic associated with North American values. In my approach to Spanish Generation X fiction within this context, however, I am aware of the homogenizing potential of the hegemonic cultural centers. My objective is not to demonstrate how Spanish fiction has succumbed to the dominant culture, but rather to show how the novelists in this study resist that dominance through a recurrent theme: a preoccupation with the diminished, destabilized, or dislocated subject in the global media and economic environment as a means of resisting and questioning rather than acquiescing in or celebrating the onslaught of signifying practices associated with the economic and cultural logic of capitalism.

1

Consuming and Communicating in the Audiovisual Environment: Ray Loriga's *La pistola de mi hermano and* José Ángel Mañas's *Historias del Kronen*

As MENTIONED IN THE INTRODUCTORY CHAPTER, THE GENERATIONAL shift in Spanish fiction in the last decade of the twentieth century can be attributed, in part, to the communication technology revolution and its ramifications in the modes of production and distribution of culture in the 1990s. The displacement of hegemonic textual language by an audiovisual mode of communication and the transformation of human experience by a globalized market and an increasingly commodified environment have all contributed to shaping the creative expression of the Spanish novelists who grew up in the information age. This chapter explores the impact of contemporary audiovisual culture and the modes of production and distribution of culture in Mañas's *Historias del Kronen* and in Loriga's *La pistola de mi hermano.*

Currently it is common for novelists to be engaged in the other forms of creative expression at the same time as they ply their trade as writers. This double vocation illustrates the breakdown of the traditional division between typographic and audiovisual expression. There are a number of film directors or screenplay writers among the Spanish Generation X novelists. The 2001 winner of the Nadal Prize, Fernando Marías, who is also a screenplay writer, drew attention to the relationship between his novel, *El niño de los coroneles* (The colonels' son), and film during the award ceremony. That same year, in what appears to be a recognition of this trend, the Destino publishing house awarded a new prize for the novel with the highest possibility of being adapted to the big screen. It was won by two novelists who are also screenplay writers, Yolanda García Serrano and Verónica Fernández, for their novel *De qué va eso del amor* (What that love thing is all about). Both Loriga and Mañas are representatives of this current close relationship between literary fiction and film. Loriga himself directed the film adaptation of *La pistola de mi hermano* in 1997. Prior to this, in 1994, Mañas set the trend in motion when he codirected the film version of *Historias del Kronen* with Montxo Armendáriz.

It has also become increasingly common for novels to be adapted to film no sooner than they are published. Three of the eight novels in this study, as well as many others attributed to this generation, have been adapted to film or are in the process of being adapted.[1] Even where novelists like Belén Gopegui are reluctant to participate on a very technical level in the transference of their novels to the screen, they are obliged to collaborate, if even on an informal level, with the directors. It appears then that the Generation X novelists, consciously or unconsciously, see themselves as being equipped to tell their story in both typographic and audiovisual formats. The narrowing of the gap between visual and typographic fiction is also evident in the fact that most Generation X novels read like movies in the first place. Gabriela Bustelo herself says that her second novel, *Planeta hembra* (Female planet), reads like a movie script. Indeed, she admits that "antes de ser libro [*Planeta hembra*] fue un tratamiento para un guión" (before it became a book, *Planeta hembra* was an outline for a movie script).[2]

La pistola de mi hermano and *Historias del Kronen* are no exceptions. Both of them mimic cinematographic language, and one feels that they were written with the future film version in mind. Both of the novels display formal and linguistic cinematographic characteristics such as the privileging of dialogue and colloquial language over narration and formal register. *Historias del Kronen*, for example, is almost entirely made up of the dialogue between the protagonist and his friends and family. The typical colloquial and vulgar tone of the novel is set in the very first words of Carlos, the narrator and protagonist: "Me jode ir al Kronen los sábados por la tarde porque está siempre hasta el culo de gente. No hay ni una puta mesa libre y hace un calor insoportable" (I fucking hate to go to the Kronen on Saturday evenings because it's fucking packed with people. There isn't a fucking table available and it's unbearably hot) (*Historias* 1994, 11). This statement, like many parts of the novel, imitates the spontaneous, oral expression of thought with which popular films evoke realism.

The few narrative portions of the novel are the first-person observations made by Carlos in the present. A typical example of this narrative technique can be found in the first paragraphs of the novel: "Roberto echa una ojeada a nuestro alrededor para ver si Pedro ha llegado. Luego, mira su reloj y dice: joder con el Pedro, desde que tiene novia pasa de todo el mundo" (Roberto takes a quick look around to see if Pedro has arrived. Then, he looks at his watch and says: fuck Pedro; he doesn't care about anyone since he got himself a girlfriend) (11). On one level, these observations read like excerpts from a director's instructions. One sees behind those words the director describing to the actors their mode of action. There are several moments in the dialogues when the narrator assumes the voice of director, such as in the following example when he interrupts his friends' conversation as they sit in the Kronen bar waiting for another friend: "Raúl y Fierro dicen que han quedado con Yoni más tarde, en Graf. Yo y Roberto protestamos inmediatamente y dejamos bien claro que nosostros pasamos de ir a Graf. Luego nos ponemos a hablar del partido y Raúl empieza a decir tonterías" (Raúl and Fierro say that they are meeting with Yoni later at Graf. Roberto and I protest immediately and make it quite clear that we are not interested in going to Graf. Then we start to talk about the game and Raúl begins to say silly things) (13).

On another level these observations can also be seen as textual renditions of visual shots. In this case Carlos's voice works like the cinematographic lens, taking in the totality of a scene or condensing a sequence of actions into one shot. Mañas manipulates the narrative voice in *Historias del Kronen* in the same way as the cameraman or camerawoman manipulates scenes by directing the viewer's attention to what is considered to be significant in the opinion of the director. In the final pages of the novel, for instance, Carlos's voice dominates entirely because he has become talkative from being under the influence of drugs and alcohol and because he tends to assume control of the others' actions; Mañas takes the liberty of suppressing all the other voices by replacing them with empty parentheses: "(   )." On occasion, what they say can be deduced from Carlos's ramblings:

¿Qué le has comprado al Fierro, Miguel? ( ) Te juro que estuve a punto de comprarle el mismo. Yo le he comprado el de Simpli Red, pero en compact. . . . ( ) Oye, ¿está muy lejos todavía la casa de Fierro? Esto está en el culo del mundo. ( ) ¿Hey, no pensáis que es una pena que Pedro se haya traído a su novia? (215)

[What did you buy for Fierro, Miguel? ( ) I swear I was about to buy him the same thing. I bought him the one by Simply Red, but on CD. . . . ( ) Listen, is it still very far to Fierro's house? This is way the hell out in the sticks. ( ) Hey, don't you think that it's a shame that Pedro brought his girlfriend?]

One can imagine that in the film, the focus of the camera would mostly be on Carlos, and the voices replaced with empty parentheses would be muted to make Carlos's stand out.

In keeping with the tendency to imitate orality and represent it audiovisually, graphics also have a semantic role to play in Mañas's novel. For example, in addition to exclamation marks, the author typographically indicates raised voices by using capital letters:

—¡CUÁNTO TIEMPO SIN VERTE! ¿CÓMO
ESTÁS? ¿QUÉ HACES AQUÍ? . . .
—¿QUÉ?
—QUE QUÉ TAL ESTÁS.
—AY, NO ME GRITES ASÍ . . .
—NO ME ESCUPAS AL OÍDO.
¿QUÉ?
—NADA. (17)
[—IT'S BEEN AGES! HOW ARE YOU?
WHAT ARE YOU DOING HERE? . . .
—WHAT?
—I SAID, HOW ARE YOU?
—OUCH! DON'T SCREAM LIKE THAT . . .
—DON'T SPIT IN MY EAR.
—WHAT?
-NOTHING.]

Another illustration of orality in *Historias del Kronen* is the phonetic transcription of some words, especially of non-Spanish nouns and Spanish translations from the English originals, as well

as the removal of the spaces between the words of a phrase in a
title:

La tele sigue encendida y la Emeteuve [MTV] pasa un vídeo de Madonna: laikaviryen [Like a virgin]. (127)

[The TV is still on and MTV is showing a Madonna video: Like a
Virgin.]

En los Renuar [Renoir] echan Rifraf [Rif Raf,], Elsilenciodeloscord-
eros [El silencio de los corderos], Lasospecha [La sospecha], Elnido-
deadán [El nido de Adán] y Ladoblevidadeverónica [La doble vida de
Verónica]. En los Alfabil [Alphaville] echan Naitonerz [Night on
Earth], y Delicatesen, Hastaelfindelmundo [Hasta el fin del mundo]
y una película de Romer: Cuentodeinvierno. [Cuento de invierno] En
sesión de madrugada: Jenriretratodeunasesino [Henry retrato de un
asesino] y Bagdadcafé [Bagadad Café]. (70)

[At the Renoir cinemas they are showing *Riff Raff, Silence of the
Lambs, Suspicion, Adam's Nest* and *The Double Life of Veronica*. The
Alphaville cinemas are showing *Night on Earth, Delicatessen, Until
the End of the World* and a Romer film: *A Tale of Winter*. For the early
morning showing: *Henry Portrait of a Serial Killer* and *Baghdad
Café*.][3]

As these examples show, most of the words transcribed in this way in
Historias del Kronen originate from popular music, television, or film.
It appears then as if Mañas disregards the conventions of writing to
reproduce phonetically the words and expressions with which his
characters must have become acquainted only aurally. Most of these
words or their translations are words that have crept into the Spanish
popular parlance through the American-dominated popular media.
Mañas could also be applying a scriptwriting technique whereby actors
are prompted to pronounce unfamiliar words, especially foreign words
with their phonetic transcriptions. Thus, in the novel some characters
are said to be wearing "Naik" (Nike) trainers (52), "Reiban" (Ray
Ban) sunglasses (52), and they drink "Huaitlabel" (White Label)
whiskey (71).

In addition to echoing the language of film and audiovisual popular
culture in general, some Generation X novels appear to be modeled
entirely on Hollywood film genres. Popular among these are the film
noirs and the road movies. In this regard, Toni Dorca has drawn atten-

tion to the similarities between *La pistola de mi hermano* and Hollywood road movies such as *Thelma and Louise:*

En ocasiones la novela se construye a partir de una película, como en
La pistola de mi hermano . . . El texto de Loriga es un refrito de los
filmes de carretera (*Corazón salvaje,* de David Lynch; *Thelma y Louise,* de Ridley Scott; y *Asesinos natos,* de Oliver Stone) construido a
base de breves fragmentos que reproducen la narración cinemato-
gráfica en secuencia. (1997, 316)

[At times the novel is modeled on a film, like *La pistola de mi hermano.* Loriga's text is a rehash of road movies (*Wild Heart,* by David
Lynch; *Thelma and Louise,* by Ridley Scott; and *Natural Born Killers,*
by Oliver Stone); it is made up of brief fragments that reproduce the
cinematographic narrative in sequence.]

In *La pistola de mi hermano* the rebel fugitives are a young man
and a young girl running away from her abusive father. The former
is on the run after killing a guard at a 7-Eleven and later killing the
attendant at a gas station. The first-person narrator of the novel
himself draws several parallels between his story and the Hollywood movies he has seen, especially *Thelma and Louise.* For instance, he compares the two policemen investigating the murders
to the "good cop/bad cop" cliché in films. He even thinks that the
seemingly empathetic police officer in this case is like Harvey Keitel who plays the role of Hal, the "good cop" in *Thelma and
Louise:*

El policía tranquilo me miró como si los dos comprendiéramos algo al
mismo tiempo. La verdad es que lo hacían bien, pero no me la daban.
Ya había visto eso en las películas. Uno hace de poli bueno y el otro
hace de poli malo. El poli malo te asusta y entonces vas tú y se lo cuen-
tas todo al poli bueno. Para que salve al chico y todo ese rollo. Como
el policía bueno de *Thelma y Louise,* el que hacía Harvey Keitel. (*La
pistola* 1995, 54–55; future references will be given parenthetically by
page number in the text)

[The quieter cop now looked at me as if there was some kind of understanding between the two of us. The truth is that they were doing a
pretty good job, but they still didn't fool me. I had seen that trick before in the movies. One plays the good cop and the other plays the bad
cop. First the bad cop scares you, and then you go and tell the whole

story to the good cop. This guy was just like the good cop in *Thelma and Louise*, Harvey Keitel's character.][4]

Apart from the various allusions that link *La pistola de mi hermano* to road movies, there are several moments in the novel that resemble film shots from that genre. For example, the narrator gives a description of the couple in flight in such a way that he captures the scene as though through the lens of a cinematographic camera. First close up when they get into the car in which they are going to flee: "[S]e subieron en el coche y arrancaron y no volvieron a mirar hacia atrás nunca más . . . Después los dos se ajustaron el cinturón de seguridad. Ella dijo: 'En estos coches europeos no hay manera de matarse'" (they got into the car and started the motor and drove off and didn't look back, not even once . . . Then they fastened their seat belts. She said: "There's no way to get killed in these European cars") (68). The next description is like a shot of them from a distance, as they drive away: "Visto desde muy atrás el trigo crecía y ellos se hacían cada vez más pequeños. Las nubes mientras tanto se parecían a todas las cosas y realmente a ninguna" (From far away, you could see the wheat field getting bigger and bigger and at the same time, the two of them getting smaller and smaller. The clouds, meanwhile, looked like lots of things, and nothing at all) (68).

Because of their seeming imitation of characters, speech, and motifs from popular film culture, critics have often seen Mañas's and Loriga's novels as merely reproducing the language and themes from television and film narratives for commercial purposes. This might appear to be the case if one were to consider these novels only superficially. After all, José Ángel Mañas's *Historias del Kronen* is populated by Spanish suburban youths who appear to be clones of similar Westernized youths the world over with no interest in Spanish national affairs or in world politics for that matter; youths whose lives appear to revolve around the consumption of drugs, designer goods, television programs, music concerts, movies, and pulp fiction. Similarly, the paperback edition of Ray Loriga's novel *La pistola de mi hermano* shows on its front cover a young man clutching a pistol, as though pandering to popular tastes in violence and spectacle. Furthermore, his characters appear to have emerged from a B road movie, violent television news, or even from television talk shows. Both authors, then, appear to be offering to their readers what Mike Featherstone has called "the spectre of cultural homogenization in the form of . . . Americanization" (1990, 10).

However, the formal and linguistic manifestations of the influence of the dominant audiovisual culture on Spanish fiction is but one aspect of the role of the latter in defining contemporary Generation X fiction. Mañas's and Loriga's novels are not mere products of their environment but also critics of it. In a self-referential sort of way, Generation X fiction deals with themes arising from the intersection between the textual and the audiovisual modes of expression. Although Mañas's main character, Carlos, insists that "La poesía . . . [e]s un género en extinción . . . Es una cultura muerta. La cultura de nuestra época es audiovisual" (Poetry . . . is becoming extinct . . . It is a dead culture. The culture of our time is audiovisual) (42), Mañas's and Loriga's novels show that they do not entirely subvert or disregard textual language as Carlos suggests. Rather, their work reflects the tension arising from the interaction between competing modes of expression. In *La pistola de mi hermano* such a tension is evident in the constant reminder of the competition between reading and watching television or movies. The narrator's brother, obviously an avid reader, reminds his younger brother that "No te das cuenta, pero leer es mejor. La televisión está bien, y sobre todo las películas *Darkman, Thelma y Louise*" (You don't know it yet, but reading's the best. TV and movies are okay, especially *Darkman, Thelma and Louise*) (22).[5] Furthermore, in his last phone call to his younger brother before being gunned down by the police, he tells him: "lee mucho y dale grasa a las botas" (read a lot, and polish your boots) (153).

Beneath the apparent dominant discourse of film and television in *La pistola de mi hermano* and *Historias del Kronen*, there is a subtext of critique in which the narrator confronts a recurrent theme in Generation X fiction: the issue of the assertion of the subject's identity in nontextual media of expression. The leitmotif running through Loriga's novel, for example, is the narrator's attempt to rescue what he deems to be the true identity of his brother from the distorted image into which it has degenerated in audiovisual media. He takes issue, especially, with the transformation of his brother from a marginalized, disaffected youth into a social deviant in order to convert him into appropriate material for the consumption of the nondiscerning, passive audience of television talk shows. Whatever complex motivations there might be behind the murder committed by his brother are totally lost in his transformation into a consumable image.[6] In the public eye his actions are attributed to his watching violent films although his brother claims that "ni siquiera iba tanto al cine" (he didn't even go to the movies that much) (17). Even policemen who are sent to investigate the crime have preconceived notions of the type of criminal they were looking for. Therefore, as the narrator points out, they both overlook his brother's library: "Ojeaba los libros con mucho interés, los otros policías habían pasado por delante de los libros como quien pasa al lado de una pared de ladrillos. Sólo querían encontrar drogas o armas o revistas de tíos desnudos" (He scanned the bookshelf with interest; the other cops had gone right past it, as if it were a brick wall. They were just looking for drugs, or weapons, or magazines with naked guys) (77–78). The prejudicial attitude of the police is not surprising given that "[l]os de la televisión lo pintaron como el loco de la tele. Ponían películas, trozos de películas, y decían que era lo mismo" (the TV reporters made him out to be some sort of TV freak. They would show short movie clips and then say he was trying to be just like *them*) (17). However, the narrator is anxious to point out that "[p]ues no señor, no lo era. Mi hermano no era un demente de esos que andan repitiendo lo que ven en el cine" (sorry, guys. Wrong again. My brother was not one of those kooks who imitate what they see in the movies) (ibid.).

Loriga's narrator, in these instances, shares Kalle Lasn's observation that in the media-dominated consumer society:

> Everything human beings once experienced directly had been turned into a representation, a show put on by someone else. Real living had been replaced by pre-packaged experiences and media-created events. Immediacy was gone. Now there was only "mediacy"—life as mediated through other instruments, life as a media creation ... [T]he spectacle had "kidnapped" our real lives, co-opting whatever authenticity we once had. (2000, 416)

For the facile consumption of a public that experiences the world audiovisually, complexity is sacrificed completely. Whatever else the murderer might be, he is represented by means of recognizable signs within the databank of stereotypes and clichés with which the public had become accustomed through spectacle. As such, the murderer's image and that of his family, as it is mediated through the circuit of television and radio talk shows, lose their complexity and context to a cliché sensationalist narrative to be consumed by the audience.

In the media format, reality loses all substance as the narrator suggests when he compares the TV talk show host to ice cream in a microwave: "Era una de esas mujeres que de ser pobre sería fea. La ropa y el maquillaje conseguían que al primer vistazo pareciera algo, pero con una segunda mirada se desvanecía como un helado en una microondas" (She was one of those women who would be ugly if she were poor. Her clothes and her makeup made her appear attractive initially. But on second glance her beauty melted away like ice cream in a microwave) (83).[7]

To heighten even further the sensational quality of the television version, the narrator and his mother are also transformed before being presented to the audience:

Mamá estaba otra vez guapísima. Nos llevaban a muchos programas porque éramos una familia muy guapa. Insistían mucho en que yo tuviera aspecto de delincuente juvenil. En la sala de maquillaje me despeinaron un poco y me cambiaron la cazadora de mi hermano por una roja más vistosa pero demasiado nueva. La presentadora le dijo a la gente que era la cazadora de mi hermano. (84)

[My mother was stunning, as usual. We went on a lot of talk shows, I think, just because we were such a good-looking family. They insisted on making me up to look like a juvenile delinquent. In the makeup room they tousled my hair and made me take off my brother's jacket and put on a brand-new red one, which was pretty cool, but definitely too new. The talk-show host said it was my brother's jacket on the air.] (Translation modified)

The narrator sums up the disjunction between the self and the media image when he explains why he no longer wanted to attend the television programs with his mother:

[Y]a no me divertía mucho con lo de la tele y la radio y los periódicos, estaba un poco cansado. De tanto hablar de él se iba convirtiendo en un desconocido. Pensé que si volvía a verle me sentiría como el hermano de una estrella de rock. Como algo que él había dejado atrás y que ya casi no recordaba. (118)

[I just wasn't having fun with it anymore; the TV, the radio and all the newspapers, I was tired of them. I had talked so much about my brother that he was turning into a stranger. I started to think, if I ever got to see him again, I'd probably feel like the brother of a rock star. Like something he'd left behind and barely remembered.] (Translation modified)

By pointing out the distortion of his brother's image through the medium of the talk shows, the narrator confronts a major question in identity formation in the dominant audiovisual culture. The contradiction between the media image and the other image seen through a brother's eyes leads one to the conclusion that the former is already processed meaning made to appear as inherent undisputable truth. Not only is meaning foisted upon the public in the process of identity formation in this environment, but the public is also made to feel as if it plays an active role in the process when in reality it does not. The media interference in determining the narrator's brother's identity in *La pistola de mi hermano* illustrates Fred Inglis's observation that "Spectacle pretends by means of its elan, vividness, domestic accessibility (sitting-room television, newspaper, radio) and power so to shape our way of seeing that we are party to what we can watch" (1988, 138).

In addition to highlighting the role of the audiovisual media in processing identity for consumption in the network consumer society, Generation X novelists also address the issue of power play between the subject and the medium. Like *La pistola de mi hermano*, *Historias del Kronen* also positions the subject within an audiovisually mediated environment. In Mañas's novel, the relationship between the subject and the dominant media of communication demonstrates how media implosion paradoxically diminishes the role of the subject in the communication process and consequently undermines fundamental human relationships. *Historias del Kronen* offers up for scrutiny extreme examples of subjects rendered powerless in their interaction with the dominant audiovisual medium of communication in a media-saturated society.

The protagonist and first-person narrator, Carlos, seems to be in constant receptive mode, to information emanating from various communication media from which he appears to derive his experiences. During a family meal the news is in the background: "Nadie

habla durante la comida porque estamos todos viendo el teledi-
ario" (Nobody talks while we eat dinner because we're watching
the news) (28). Shortly after this meal, he is to be found in his
bedroom listening to a CD, while his brother is in the living room
watching television. That very afternoon he watches his favorite
video "Jenriretratodeunasesino" (30), a film he watches every
other day according to one of his friends. In fact there are very
few moments of intimate communication in the novel. Even when
Carlos goes to have lunch with his ailing grandfather, he says "yo
miro la televisión mientras como. El viejo ha dejado de comer y
sólo bebe mientras prosigue su monólogo" (I watch television
while I eat. The old man has stopped eating and only drinks while
he carries on his monologue) (84). It is evident that Carlos's experience of reality at various levels, whether love, friendship, sex, or
violence, is filtered through one form or other of audiovisual spectacle. This includes rock concerts like the Elton John concert he
attended with Amalia (152–59); CDs of music by the *Ramones,
Paralisis Permanente, Paralisis Total,* and other bands of the
1980s that were associated with the Madrid counterculture known
as the "movida"; pornographic movies; violent movies; or even the
news. By all indications, therefore, Carlos and his friends inhabit
a world such as the one Jean Baudrillard describes as "the fragmented, filtered world, the world reinterpreted in terms of this
simultaneously technical and 'legendary' code, that we 'consume'—the entire material of the world, the whole of culture industrially processed into finished products, into sign material,
from which all eventual, cultural or political value has vanished"
(1998, 124). Within this environment, two-way communication is
impossible. As Lasn correctly observes, "[in] our media-saturated
postmodern world . . . all communication flows in one direction,
from the powerful to the powerless" (2000, 418). What this means
is that within this media-dominated environment, Carlos and his
friends receive, rather than create, already-made messages. Their
experience is "'consumable' . . . reworked by a whole industrial
chain of production—the mass media—into a finished product, a
material of combined, finite signs, analogous to the finished products of industrial production" (Baudrillard 1998, 125–26).

   The manner in which Carlos experiences reality makes him unable to engage in deep human relationships and makes him reject
any form of mutual interaction. His preference for received mean-

ing over bilateral communication is evident in the manner in which he avoids conversation, especially any form of conversation that does not imitate the violent interaction that he is used to seeing in films and on television. When he goes out for a meal with an old friend, Nuria, he abandons her in the restaurant complaining that "[y]a he aguantado suficientes sermones por hoy. Estoy harto de que todo el mundo se dedique a decirme lo que tengo que hacer" [I have tolerated enough sermons for today. I am fed up with everyone telling me what I have to do) (149). Interestingly, he ends up instead in a mall, alone, watching a South American soap opera (150). As he finds that to be equally boring, he quickly phones another friend to make a date to see an Elton John concert. It is as though Carlos flees intimate conversation or communication to make himself available to the assault of the spectacle on his senses and this in turn conditions his relationship with people.

The question of the significance of communication and the consequences of its absence becomes the focus of discussion on one occasion when another friend, Amalia, refuses to engage in one of his games of sexual control, preferring instead to engage him in conversation. To this Carlos protests angrily: "Hablar, hablar. Lo que queréis todos siempre es hablar, hablar, hablar y hablar. No os dais cuenta de que hay gente que prefiere no hablar, que no lo racionaliza todo, que prefiere la emoción a la lógica, que prefiere el instinto a la razón" (Talk, talk. What you all want always is to talk, talk, talk and talk. You don't realize that there are people who prefer not to talk, who don't rationalize everything, who prefer emotion to logic, who prefer instinct to reason) (169). In these words, Carlos underlines his relationship with the media through which he experiences reality. The media make the signs, the images, the conclusion, seem natural; rather like what ideologies do, according to T. J. Clark: "they present constructed and disputable meanings as if they were hardly meanings at all, but, rather forms inherent in the world-out-there which the observer is privileged to intuit directly" (1985, 8). Carlos's rejection of poetry when he says "[l]a poesía es sentimental, críptica y aburrida . . . Es un género en extinción" (poetry is sentimental, cryptic and boring . . . It is a genre that is becoming extinct) (42), is in keeping with his abhorrence of letters and by extension of words and direct human communication: "Carlos odia las cartas. Dice que son anacrónicas y que sólo los sentimentales escriben cartas" (Carlos hates letters.

He says that they are anachronistic and that only sentimental people write them) (230). In poetry and in letters, unlike in the popular media-generated genres, meaning is not pre-scripted, and the
writer or the sender has to put himself or herself in the communicative, not the receptive, mode to read or write them.

Interestingly the only textual mode of communication that Carlos does not reject is Bret Easton Ellis's *American Psycho*. This
novel's main character, Patrick Bateman, is his hero and role
model. *American Psycho* appeals to Carlos and his friends' obsession with violence in the media. The graphic descriptions of gratu-
itous, abstracted, violent acts committed by Bateman appeal to
their senses, which are so conditioned by violence packaged to
produce a predetermined effect in music and film. As Carlos finds
himself assailed by macabre thoughts of violence, he begins to
wonder what it would feel like to commit murder. He smiles to
himself as he remembers that "[s]egún Beitman, es como un subi-
dón de adrenalina brutal, como una primera raya" (according to
Bateman, it is like a wild rush of adrenaline, like a first fix) (134).
The spectacle of violence, like the narcotic, is beyond the control
of its recipient; its message is ingrained directly on the brain of the
latter without the possibility of mediation. To a great extent, Carlos is like his hero Bateman whose violence, according to James
Annesley, is fueled by his

> [I]nability to relate to any kind of reality. His daily encounters with
> computer screens spilling digits with only a tenuous connection to the
> concrete values they represent, has created, in terms of the novel, a
> sense of financial and material unreality that weakens his grip on the
> real. The result is that Bateman becomes unable to see his actions in
> anything other than in fictional terms. Thus in the same way that his
> manipulations of money are separated from the material realities they
> represent, his violence seems equally unconnected to either human ex-
> periences or humanity. (1998, 17–18)

Carlos and his friends seem to have undergone a similar disconnection from reality. This is confirmed when they turn a birthday
party into a sadomasochistic game that ends with the death of the
host, Fierro. Under Carlos's directions, they tie up Fierro and force
a whole bottle of whiskey down his throat. They do this because,
according to Carlos, Fierro would enjoy the sadomasochistic thrill.
Carlos completely ignores protests by Fierro, a diabetic, and urges

his friends on. As is to be expected, Carlos is thrilled himself that this game "[p]arece una película, ¿verdad? Es como Nuevesemanasymedia [Nueve semanas y media]" (looks like a movie, doesn't it? It's like *Nine and a Half Weeks*) (221). Furthermore, when things take a turn for the worse he is unable to appreciate the human tragedy that has just occurred and rather gets even more violent and chastises the rest of the men for being "unos débiles" (a bunch of wimps) (223). The whole incident, and most of the party for that matter, is reported through Carlos's direct speech with other people's replies and comments suggested in empty parentheses. It is noteworthy that once again importance is placed not on exchange and communication but on the spectacle. For Carlos then, the incident has the same value as the violent fictions he has been watching or reading: *American Psycho, The Clockwork Orange* and the mythical "snuff movies."

Roberto, who gives the incident more thought, rightfully confesses to a psychiatrist that "[t]odo aquel rollo que llevábamos nos embruteció tanto que a nadie le pareció rara la idea de Carlos. Yo creo que si Carlos nos hubiera propuesto matarle, tampoco nos hubiera extrañado nada" (all that nonsense we were involved in had brutalized us so much that no one found Carlos's idea strange. I believe that if Carlos had proposed that we kill him it would not have shocked us either) (237). Roberto realizes that the proliferation of the spectacle, and audiovisual communication in particular, had devalued concrete human references and replaced them with an increased incidence of simulations and packaged visual codes. According to him, this is what Carlos appears to be suggesting when he compares reality to the movies (237). It is also the end result of the situation in which the audiovisual spectacle serves to "neutralize the lived, unique, eventual character of the world and substitute for it a multiple universe of media which, as such, are homogenous one with another" (Baudrillard 1998, 123). Carlos and his friends, who do not communicate but receive meaning all the time through the mass media, receive reality constantly as a "consumable" filtered, fragmented, and reworked product completely detached from external human interaction and experience. And this explains the emptiness in which they live.

Consuming information rather than communicating is but one aspect of the audiovisual consumer society that Generation X writers deal with in their novels. In both Mañas's and Loriga's novels, consumerism is as central to the significance of the novels as is the understanding of the audiovisual media environment in which they are set. The characters are as much victims of the onslaught of spectacle as they are of ubiquitous commodification. Furthermore, both novels seem to be so self-conscious of their location within the consumer culture that it would be impossible to consider these texts without locating them in this particular cultural and economic context.

The principal spaces of action in both *La pistola de mi hermano* and *Historias del Kronen* are less spaces of communing, such as the home or the workplace, and more spaces of consuming such as malls, bars, and concerts. In *Historias del Kronen,* especially, the home is but a transitory space with a network of highways taking the characters away from it to the spaces of consumption. Carlos's itinerary and his disconnection from the spaces of communing are illustrated in these excerpts from chapters 3 and 4 of the novel:

Durante la comida, la gorda me recuerda que hoy es el cumpleaños del viejo y que habrá que regalarle algo. Como cada año, decidimos comprarle unos libros de poesía y quedamos para ir a Hiperión por la tarde. (38–39)

[At lunch, Fatty reminds me that it's the old man's birthday today and we have to give him something. As we do every year we decide to give him some books of poetry and we agree to go to Hiperión in the evening.]

Salimos por la Nacionaluno [Nacional uno] con dirección a Burgos. Pasado Alcobendas, empieza a haber indicaciones de Iteuve [ITV] a seis kilómetros. (40)

[We take the Nacional Uno highway toward Burgos. After Alcobendas we begin to see signs indicating that there is an ITV six kilometers away.]

Bajamos hasta la Puerta de Alcalá andando. Pasamos Serrano y tomamos la primera bocacalle a la derecha hasta llegar a la librería Hiperión. (41)

[We walk down to Puerta de Alcalá. We pass Serrano street and turn right at the first intersection and walk till we get to Hiperión bookstore.]

Oye, yo voy a tener que pasarme por el Kronen que he quedado con los otros. (59)

[Listen, I am going to have to go through Kronen 'cos I'm meeting the others there.]

Hola, loco, ponme un Jotabé con cocacola. (62)
[Hey, dude, give me a J&B with Coke.]

The ubiquity of consuming is further illustrated by the fact that most of the characterization in both novels is achieved through what the characters purchase, wear, drink or listen to. The brother of the narrator in *La pistola de mi hermano* is identified by his clothes: a pair of tight black jeans and snakeskin boots—clothes that identify him with youth rebellion. The narrator himself informs the reader that one of the moments of fraternal bonding between him and his brother involves a visit to the mall to purchase CDs: "En lo de los discos éramos uno, nos gustaba exactamente lo mismo, . . . Teníamos poco dinero y nos llevamos sólo el último de Nirvana" (When it came to music, we liked exactly the same things . . . We were broke that day, so we only got the latest Nirvana CD) (30). Interestingly, the youth in *Historias del Kronen* are identified by similar music labels that mark them all as products of MTV.

Significantly, in these novels "being" is displaced by "having" and people do not simply wear clothes but rather brands: "Esperamos un rato y, al cabo, Miguel sale del portal . . . Miguel lleva pantalones cortados, botas Naik negras de raper y gafas de sol Reiban de piloto de avión" [We wait a bit and after a while Miguel walks through the front door . . . Miguel is wearing shorts, black Nike rapper boots and Ray-Ban pilot sunglasses) (52). What is more, a similar observation has been made by Annesley regarding *American Psycho:*

These mechanisms can be traced by reflecting on blank fiction's constant allusions to retail outlets, brand names and styles. Bret Easton Ellis's novels typify this kind of approach. His characters don't drive cars, they drive "BMWs," they don't eat in restaurants, they eat in "Spago's," they don't wear sunglasses, they wear "Raybans" . . . Blank fiction does not just depict its own period, it speaks in the commodified language *of* its own period. (1998, 7)

The allusion to commodities in these novels also reflects a neutralizing trend in contemporary culture, which spells the disappearance of national identity. National popular cultural specificity has given way to hegemonic American culture. In both novels, the characters drink the same beverages, such as Coca-Cola; they listen to the same kind of music or refer to the same kinds of music and musicians. The phenomenon is similar to that observed by the first-person narrator in Douglas Coupland's novel *Generation X* in reference to the consumer culture of the nineties: "but where you're from feels sort of irrelevant these days ('since everyone has the same stores in their mini malls,' according to my younger brother, Tyler)" (1991, 4). The same commodities and icons that one would find in American fictions of the same generation appear in Mañas's and Loriga's novels.

Mañas and Loriga rely so heavily on the language of commodity culture for meaning that one wonders if their works are mere commodities themselves or whether, as is being suggested in this study, they represent a critique of the commodity culture. For example, one wonders, as does Annesley with regard to *American Psycho*, whether with the proliferation of brand names in these novels these authors are merely paying homage to the capitalist god of their creation by engaging in the marketing strategy of commodity placement. Their novels, thus spluttered with references to recognizable brand names can be seen as directed toward a readership that is only loyal to that which chronicles or reflects, in no uncertain terms, its vital space. I depart from the inquiry into the authorial intention in this matter to suggest that the relationship between these Generation X novels and the consumer culture is an ambiguous one.

La pistola de mi hermano and *Historias del Kronen* undermine the traditional sublime status of creative culture by revealing their close association with the consumer society in their language and themes. In this way, both draw attention to one of the fundamental features of postmodern literature, which, according to Fredric Jameson, is "the effacement in them of . . . the frontier between high culture and so-called mass or commercial culture (1990, 2). Quite like fiction revealing itself to be nothing but fiction, these novels problematize the opposition between literature and commodity by flaunting the hitherto hidden artifacts of the modes of production and distribution in representations through fiction.

Their relationship to the cultural context is akin to what Baudrillard says of pop art: they regard themselves as "homogenous with their industrial, mass production and hence with the artificial manufactured character of the whole environment" (Baudrillard 1998, 115). The contemporary mode of production determines their content and their language and as such plays a role in sealing their intimate association with the consumer culture. As Baudrillard says "it is not sufficient to change the content of the picture or the artist's intentions: it is the structures of the production of culture which decide the matter. Ultimately, only the rationalization of the art market, on the same basis as any other industrial market, could desacralize artworks and restore them to the status of everyday objects" (1998, 119). Generation X novels are doubly desacralized because their authors consciously position them in that rationalized market from which they have no escape.

The publishing industry has not been immune to the economic imperatives and marketing strategies adopted by secular industries. Subsequently, the industry's quest for higher returns, wider readership, and its employment of the media and other marketing tools to achieve its financial goals have played a significant role in the formation of this generation of writers. This cohort of writers tends to be constituted by, to borrow from Baudrillard, "a *simulation*, a 'consommé' of the [global] signs" (1998,101) of youth in the nineties and as such their differences as a result of their varied aesthetic and ideological conventions tend to be overlooked. Their publishers adopted the marketing strategy of name recognition and proceeded to market the new generation by labeling them in media-friendly terms through images that exploited the marketing advantages of linking the writers with a readership with which the former supposedly shared an identity. The Generation X novelists are not the first age-identified generation of writers in Spanish literary history. They were preceded at the beginning of the twentieth century by no less than the Generation of 1927. Rafael Alberti of that generation published his first collection of poems at the age of twenty-three. However, this nineties generation of young writers is the first to gain immediate recognition as an age cohort due, to a great extent, to the media and the publishing industry's intervention. To their advantage however, under the patronage of the industry, the young writers have been able to break down the exclusionary barriers of the literary establishment.

On the other hand, media and commercial intervention have also contributed to alienating the group and casting doubt on their literary value. To some critics this group has been adopted, named, and marketed by publishing agencies in league with the media, as they would any other cultural artifact. As a result, some see the group more as a market category than as a literary generation. There is no doubt that the popularization of Mañas, Loriga, and their contemporaries as a generation was made possible, in part, because of the commodification of youth culture in the first place. This younger group of novelists are best located in the globalized context dominated by North American culture. In this age of globalized media-dominated culture and rapidly disseminated information, Mañas's and Loriga's novels were immediately identified with signs of youth culture, which, like other modes of identification in the consumer age, according to Baudrillard, "are laid down in advance by *models* produced industrially by mass media and composed of *identifiable* signs" (1998, 96). By the time Loriga and Mañas published their first novels, Douglas Coupland's *Generation X: Tales for an Accelerated Culture* (1991), for example, had already established the notion of the existence of a young generation whose values, unlike those of their parents' (the "baby-boom" generation) is not a purely North American phenomenon. In this age of global marketing, it was necessary to convert Mañas and his contemporaries into an item of identifiable exchange value: youth.

Youth was a product that was required to sell Spanish Generation X books. For the first time in cultural history, a literary generation was born, not only as a consequence of a departure from preexisting modes of expression, but also as a result of technological shifts in the mode of production and distribution of literature. Mañas and Loriga are not the first young writers in the literary history of Spain. However, they are the first to gain notoriety as such within the mainstream of the literary environment. Both Mañas and Loriga were promoted by publishers like Destino and Plaza y Janés, respectively. Also, members of this generation have been recipients of prestigious literary awards. Mañas's *Historias del Kronen* (1994) was short-listed for the Nadal Prize, and it marked a shift in the literary trends and established him and his generation as a force to reckon with in Spanish literature. Subsequently, other members of his generation have won the Nadal:

Pedro Maestre in 1996 with *Matando dinosaurios con tirachinas*, Lucía Etxebarria in 1997 with *Beatriz y los cuerpos celestes*, and Lorenzo Silva in 2000 with *El alquimista impaciente*.

Finally, the economic considerations behind the incursions of the publishing industry into the film industry cannot be disregarded when one considers that *Historias del Kronen*, whose cinematographic adaptation was highly successful, sold more than 80,000 copies. The sheer magnitude of these filmic adaptations and their timing have prompted critics to see them as marketing strategies adopted to boost the sale of the novels. Some of the novelists themselves have admitted to having been obliged to work as screenwriters in order to earn a living.

What is clear from the foregoing observations on *Historias del Kronen* and *La pistola de mi hermano*, however, is that their authors are conscious of their location in the media and consumer environment. Mañas and Loriga, therefore, do not merely absorb and reflect that environment but rather reveal the challenges that it poses to them as subjects desiring to be autonomous. The information technology revolution into which they were born allows them to operate within both audiovisual and textual media to meet their artistic and economic objectives. Although Loriga and Mañas use the interpenetration of the two media of communication innovatively and creatively, they also reveal, through the experiences of their central characters, the price that is paid for total subjection to the culture of spectacle and commodity: the loss of complexity and agency. This is evident in the control that the media exerts over the identity of the narrator's brother (*La pistola de mi hermano*) and in the outcome of Carlos's (*Historias del Kronen*) replacement of communication with frenetic consumption of popular culture. Indeed, the role of the media in the birth of a group of writers known as Generation X, whose identity is often tied to the audiovisual consumer culture, could be seen as being analogous to the role of the media in molding the image of Loriga's character for public consumption. This generation, as illustrated through the two novels examined here, however, asserts its agency by consciously writing within and against the contemporary media-dominated consumer culture of the nineties.

2

Urban Fictions/Popular Fictions: Gabriela Bustelo's *Veo veo* and Ismael Grasa's *De Madrid al cielo*

IT IS EVIDENT FROM THE DISCUSSION OF *HISTORIAS DEL KRONEN* AND *La pistola de mi hermano* in the preceding chapter that cinema, television, and other popular media of communication occupy a central place in Spanish Generation X fiction. They serve as sources of cultural codes and narrative discourses as well as social and ideological references. The rapprochement of novels such as José Ángel Mañas's and Ray Loriga's and cinema and television has contributed to their being dismissed by skeptics as mere extensions of the entertainment industry in which they are inspired in the first place. One cannot entirely disregard the possible considerations of marketing and accessible entertainment behind this propensity toward visual and popular genres. However, they do not adequately explain this tendency in most of the writers. Violence, street language, allusions to popular genres, commodity culture and the focus on the prosaic urban experience conceal a concern with the diminution of agency and identity in the socioeconomic and media-dominated environment of the last decade of the twentieth century.

In *Veo veo* and *De Madrid al cielo* Gabriela Bustelo and Ismael Grasa ingeniously adapt the detective genre to show how agency is undermined by the changing parameters of urban space in 1990s Spain. Both novels illustrate the breakdown of the symbiotic relationship between subject and city as a reflection of the subject's destabilization due to economic and technological changes in the urban environment.[1] I begin with an analysis of Ismael Grasa's approach to film noir in *De Madrid al cielo*. The study of Grasa's novel, according to the theories of the film noir genre shows that the profound ontological preoccupations expressed in his narrative are compatible with the existential dimension of the said popular urban genre. Through the discourse of the film noir genre, Grasa communicates his central character's sense of vulnerability resulting from his alienation from the socioeconomic order of 1990s Spain.

The protagonist of *De Madrid al cielo,* Zenón, narrates in the first person a detective story of urban violence in which a young prostitute and heroin addict, Paula, is found murdered in his bed. A friend of his, Chule, is arrested for the crime. Zenón is therefore obliged to take on the role of detective in order to, first of all, find the real murderer and second, to clear his friend's name as well as his own.

In keeping with the conventions of the film noir genre, this story is rooted in a self-conscious way in the clichés of popular crime fiction. One quickly recognizes in Grasa's novel the adaptations of various distinct elements of detective film. The iconographic, stylistic and narrative characteristics that lend to the film noir genre its unmistakable pessimism are present in various forms in *De Madrid al cielo.* Zenón, like the noir detectives, frequents or inhabits places that highlight his personality as a solitary and vulnerable individual. He lives alone in a bachelor apartment located between a dilapidated loft and the apartment of a hostile couple. When Zenón is not at home, he can be found either at a bar patronized by pimps and drug addicts or wandering on the streets of his neighborhood without attempting to establish close relationships with anyone. Furthermore, Zenón, a ragman on the verge of becoming homeless because he cannot pay his rent, is motivated to act more by his basic needs than by moral ideals. Film noir is full of similar characters: vulnerable protagonists, detectives or narrators with ambiguous moral values, such as Walter Neff (*Double Indemnity*), an insurance salesman driven by greed and adultery from the orderly world of middle-class values to commit a heinous crime; Dixon Steele (*In a Lonely Place*), a down-on-his-luck screenplay writer whose own moral instability and violent personality make him the principal suspect in a murder case; or Bradford Galt (*The Dark Corner*), whose image as a tough detective, in reality, hides his profound anguish.

Furthermore, Zenón adopts the first-person retroactive narrative form to tell his story. This narrative style is a textual adaptation of the superimposed narrative voice characteristic of the film noir genre. It makes the narrated events appear to precipitate inexorably toward a predetermined end and therefore tends to magnify the narrator's own fatalistic vision. In addition, the urban environment in *De Madrid al cielo* is analogous to the nightmarish ambience typical of the genre, which is described by Raymond Chandler as "a world gone wrong" (1972, viii). As in film noir the story told by Zenón takes place in a city in which nothing appears to fit in its expected place. Zenón's Madrid is not the next best thing to heaven, as is suggested by the popular saying,"De Madrid al cielo," which is also the title of the novel. It is hell on earth.

The selection of this genre in particular as a model for Grasa's novel is best understood if one refers to the theories that define not only the formal features of the noir genre, but also the sensibilities that they convey. In Roberto Porfirio's opinion, the pessimistic vision of the noir films "is nothing less than an existential attitude towards life" (1996, 117). Existentialism, according to Porfirio, "is an outlook which begins with a disoriented individual facing a confused world that he cannot accept. It places its emphasis on man's contingency in a world where there are no transcendental values or moral absolutes, a world devoid of any meaning but the one man himself creates" (ibid., 118). In Porfirio's view, the noir protagonist operates within a vital framework similar to the one perceived by Sartre's existentialist, Roquentin, in that revealing moment as the latter stood before the roots of the chestnut tree. As he contemplated the roots before him, reality, stripped of all imposed order, became reduced, in his eyes, to a monstrous and chaotic mass (Sartre 1966, 180). Unable to rely on order and reason, Roquentin surrenders to the power of fate in his existence as he succinctly explains: "L'éssentiel c'est la contingence . . . Exister, c'est être là , simplement" (The essential thing is contingency . . . To exist is simply to be there) (185).[2] In other words, the subject who is conscious of the limitations of the rational and the culture of the rational in determining the self and its surroundings surrenders to the absurd represented by fate. Thus, contingency, rather than rational processes, is the essential driving force within several film noirs. As the protagonist of *Detour* remarks with respect to the characteristic law of fate or destiny that governs the genre, "some day fate, or some myste-

rious force, can put the finger on you or me for no reason at all"
(quoted in Porfirio 1996, 125).

This sense of the absurd in life and the pessimism that it brings
about in the genre is appropriated by Grasa in order to underline
the following themes in *De Madrid al cielo:* the meaninglessness
of life, the negation of expectations, and the weakening of the control that the subject is expected to exercise over its own life. In
the neoliberal, market-dominated Madrid of the 1990s, Zenón, an
unemployed communist sympathizer, finds himself to be out of
place. His confidence in the knowledge of himself and of his environment is eroded with the failure of his political ideals and his
own personal failure in the new economic order. In concrete terms
Zenón expresses his feeling of dislocation and instability in the
new socioeconomic environment by focusing on what he perceives
to be the undermining of his identity as a male, his subjection to
fate, and his existence in a city that is alien to him. He is able to
do this by viewing his experiences through the discourse of the
noir film.

Zenón's preoccupation with his gender identity is illustrated in
his obsession with stories of male failure. An example of such a
story in the novel is that of the son of the bar owner in whose establishment the central events of this novel begin. This young man
became a "torero," the prime vocation of the stereotype of the Iberian male, with the suggestive nickname "Machete." Contrary to
expectations, the very day on which he was to become a fully qual-
ified bullfighter, a rather fierce bull made him lose his liking for the
sport. As a consequence he resigned himself to the not so laudable
job, according to the male ethic, of "repartidor de prensa" (newspaper delivery boy (*De Madrid* 1994, 27; future references will be
given parenthetically by page number in the text). Machete's failure is but one example of a general situation from Zenón's point
of view. His first-person narration is filled with men like himself
whose reality refutes the traditional notions of masculinity. In fact,
Machete's predicament is a reflection of Zenón's own sense of failure as a male in the Spain of the 1990s. His acute awareness of the
vulnerability of his gender and a sense of the loss of male superiority is the driving force behind this crime story.

Zenón appears to suffer from the anxiety of the postmodern
male whose self-determination in factors like professional success,
gender superiority, and the possession of firm and absolute politi-

cal ideologies is no longer possible because of transformations in the social, political, and economic structures around him. For example, he cannot claim to have control of himself and his environment when he realizes to his dismay that the alternatives to the sociopolitical norms that he himself had chosen as a communist are no longer valid. Zenón used to be a young left-wing activist who would go with his friends to "las manifestaciones a darnos de hostias con los grises en la Complutense" (the demonstrations and fight with the cops at the University) (13), and who used to sing "las canciones más bonitas y más comprometidas" (the most beautiful politically engaged songs) (ibid.). Today he finds himself without a job and almost without a roof over his head in a capitalist Madrid that is also supposedly democratic. His efforts as a political activist have been of no use at all to him. In fact, in a Madrid that he sarcastically describes as "Madrid Republicano" (Republican Madrid), he is the one who appears to be out of place. He is rather like a remnant of an antiquated ideology. Zenón, the former activist who has gone from being an itinerant bolero singer to becoming a ragman, and who is suffering an identity crisis of the male, decries these personal vicissitudes when he complains that "nadie me reconoce ahora por mi trabajo" (these days I get no recognition for my work) (29).

Far from being a bold activist effecting change, Zenón is an anachronistic communist who is practically and symbolically relegated to the margins of society. His failure and alienation is all the more evident when he compares himself to friends who abandoned the struggle for social justice to ingratiate themselves with the controllers of production. While he barely makes ends meet, these friends live in the lap of the benefits of capitalism. A case in point is that of the two friends to whom he goes in search of the fifty thousand pesetas that he needs to pay his rent. One of them, a former comrade in the Communist Party, lives in an apartment whose lobby "parecía la recepción de un hotel" (looked like the lobby of a hotel) (18) and to which one went by an elevator which was "tan grande y tan profundo que cabía un ataúd de largo" (so huge that a coffin would fit in it lengthwise) (19). Zenón, in sharp contrast to his former comrades, does not have a concrete position in his society, and this is reflected symbolically in his lack of a stable job and place of residence. In other words, both materially and ontologically, Zenón has no place within the current order.

Zenón, as well as other men in the novel, demonstrate characteristics of film noir protagonists who are described by Frank Krutnik as "hero-figures who manifest one form or another of 'problematised'—eroded or unstable—masculinity" (1991, 85).[3] Evidently, Zenón is in dire straits. He does not even have the means to put together the fifty thousand pesetas that he requires to pay his rent. At the time of the crime, he had given up his vocation as an itinerant bolero singer to earn his living as a ragman. He goes from one empty house to the other collecting discarded books and furniture in order to sell them in other neighborhoods. The image of the ragman going in and out of dilapidated empty spaces is symbolic of the ruinous state of both the character and his environment. It also suggests the erosion of the character's dignity as a person and, in Zenón's case, as a man.

Furthermore, as a detective, Zenón is more a pathetic figure than an admirable one. The noir genre detective, like Zenón, questions rather than reaffirms the male image and ethic. In *Double Indemnity*, for example, the model of masculine morality and ethics is upturned by Keyes. Keyes is the insurance claims investigator who prided himself on his ability to detect any fraudulent claims through rationalization and the study of statistics. However, these supposed abilities fail him in his investigation of the death of Mr. Dietrichson. In *De Madrid al cielo* it is even worse. Zenón attempts to portray himself as a confident detective, but he fails terribly. He instead comes across as an inept detective whose attempts at solving the crime by following clues are no more than caricatures of the actions of the careful, rational, and morally upright person. Consequently Zenón's attempt to confront his first suspect, his landlady's brother, turns out to be comical, as he displays neither confidence nor expertise in his actions. He obtains his first clue by blackmailing his neighbor; then he follows the suspect to the Ateneo de Madrid and succeeds only in leaving a ridiculous anonymous note, which does nothing to intimidate his suspect. In any case, the suspect guesses right away who the source of the note is. Zenón's efforts are not rewarded. On the contrary, he ends up being humiliated and on the street once again where he has to beg for money to buy food.

In the same noir genre the femme fatale plays an important role in revealing the vulnerability of the male figure. Paula is the femme fatale in Zenón's story. Contrary to the general image of such a character, she is not an evil woman but rather a victim. This young character is in fact a prostitute exploited by her pimp, who is also Zenón's friend. He is the same person who murders her in the end. From Zenón's perspective, however, Paula is partly responsible for the destruction of his sense of male domination. In reality, she is only a reflection of Zenón's own anxiety and obsession with his loss of prestige and security as a man. In her study of variants of the contemporary femme fatale, Kate Stables writes that in the film noirs, especially in the recent ones, they represent

> [T]he profound threat to patriarchy posed by industrial, social and cultural changes at this point in time . . . [T]oday's deep crisis of masculinity is eminently visible in popular culture, and nowhere more marked than around the *femme fatale*. Mass-market cinema has a unique ability to reflect insecurities in the male image, and the *femme fatale* figure which combines sadistic and masochistic male fantasies is a potent lightning rod for male anxieties. (1996, 166)

In the following Zenón presents Paula to the reader, and it confirms the observations made by critics on the femme fatale:

> Paula era una mujer capaz de confundir a los hombres, eso es lo que era. El macho por la mañana se ciñe el pantalón y sin vacilar orienta su picha como los toreros hacia uno u otro lado de la pernera; anda muy seguro entre las hembras hasta que da con una que le dice "por ahí", y va el macho y cuando llega ve que ella está en otro lado diciendo "por allá", y vuelve el macho a embestir humillando y barriendo el suelo con el morro. (30)

> [Paula was a woman who could mess with a guy's head; that's for sure. A man puts on his pants in the morning and with the assuredness of a torero adjusts his dick to one side in his pant leg; he goes about confidently among the females until he comes across one who says to him "this way"; but when he gets there he realizes that she is standing elsewhere saying "that way"; and he charges again like a bull with its head bowed and its mouth sweeping the dust.]

Zenón projects onto Paula a fear and an anxiety around losing his male superiority, which is seen throughout the novel in his portrayal of other women. A case in point is the married couple in his apartment building. The husband has a job that is not considered at all masculine in the patriarchal order: he sells cosmetics and he appears to live in the shadow of his tyrannical wife. According to Zenón, whenever he meets the man alone on the stairs, they greet each other; however, whenever the latter is with his wife "él no se atreve a decir ni mu porque es un hombre muy sumiso a las determinaciones de su parienta" (he does not dare say a word because he is a man who is controlled by his wife) (15–16). Other men, such as his two former comrades, are presented under the "control" of their wives. One of them, who in the past "se emborrachaba a diario" (would get drunk daily) (22) with Zenón and with whom he spent his youth engaging in "hazañas políticas de veinteañeros bocazas e insolentes" (the political exploits of insolent, bigmouthed twenty-year-olds) (23), is now completely domesticated by his life as a married man. Such is the transformation in this friend that Zenón does not dare ask him for the fifty thousand pesetas that he had gone to borrow from him in the first place. He makes his way to the house of the other friend only to find that his wife does not even allow them to meet. While reflecting on the "control" that this friend's wife exerts on him he laments that:

> El varón es un cometa y la hembra es una jirafa que te atrapa al vuelo. Las cosas son así. Al comienzo avergüenza un poco reconocerlo. (17)

> [The male is like a kite and the female is the giraffe that catches it in flight. That's how it is. At first, it is a little embarrassing to admit it.]

There is another dimension to the threat to Zenón's sense of self-worth beyond the femme fatale's seductive power and her wiliness. Although film noirs appear to focus on the latter effect, the fatal woman can also be perceived, as does Zenón, as the instrument of destiny that undermines the hapless male's ability to control the events in his life. For example, there is no doubt about the effect that the image of Mrs. Dietrichson, standing at the top of the stairs, covered only in a towel, has on Walter Neff in *Double Indemnity*. The impact that the presence of Cora, an attractive but miserable woman living with a vulgar husband at the height of the depression, has on Frank Chambers in *The Postman Always*

Rings Twice is also obvious. However, in addition to their seductive role, these women represent an element of fate in the story; they appear without any concrete reason in the logic of the story and upturn the anticipated order of events. Both Cora and Mrs. Dietrichson are like irrational destiny, which changes the course of one's life and converts two men, who are otherwise very ordinary men, into murderers. Such is the case for Walter Neff, an innocuous insurance salesman, and Frank Chambers, one of the many vagabonds created by the Depression.

In a similar fashion, Paula's presence in the novel confirms Zenón's fatalistic theory on life: "[E]s un tambor de pistola pero también es una ruleta de azar, un tiovivo de caballos, una noria de feria y también de sacar agua" (It is the drum of a revolver, but it is also like a game of chance, a merry-go-round, a ferris wheel or a waterwheel) (127). His inability to exercise control over his destiny is revealed through Paula, the personification of his vulnerability to fate. In fact, meeting Paula is what changes the course of his life. When all is said and done, before he was introduced to her, he appeared resigned to living his life as it was. However, fate in the form of Paula intervened to take him along unexpected paths.

Zenón's existential crisis in *De Madrid al cielo* is reflected not only through his diminished male superiority and his sense of being subjected to the power of fate but also through his inability to know his physical environment intimately and interpret it adequately. Zenón's perception of the city as an incoherent space is portrayed through the schism that is seen between the Madrid that he inhabits and the suggestions of a traditional or folkloric Madrid in the novel. It is also seen through his focus on images of disjunction between the city and the people who inhabit it. Like Zenón's Madrid, the urban setting of American film noirs is also marked by contradictions. The incoherence of the urban environment in this genre is attributed to the paradoxical coexistence in the same city of a stratum of progress and prosperity and another of crime and delinquency (Brand 1990, 224). There is a similar social discrepancy in *De Madrid al cielo*. In a sense, the contrasting representations of the city in Grasa's novel mirrors the discrepancy between the supposed affluence enjoyed in 1990s neoliberal Madrid and the harsh socioeconomic reality of people like Zenón who inhabit the margins.

De Madrid al cielo takes place in a Madrid with recognizable cultural and historical points of reference. A close look at the streets along which Zenón walks in his daily quests for survival shows that they are located in the area of Madrid known as the "barrios bajos" (the lower quarters). These are areas in which one finds the most authentic neighborhoods of the city. In fact, Zenón's apartment and scene of the murder is located on Cabestreros Street in Embajadores. This street is described in the *Diccionario General de Madrid* (General Dictionary of Madrid) as "una de las calles más características de Madrid castizo y barriobajero (one of the most typical and traditional streets of lower-quarter Madrid) (Montero Alonso 1990, 88).[4] However, the pure or authentic image of the city in Grasa's Madrid is as false as the suggestion of affluence and prosperity is in the American film noirs.

As Zenón unravels the mystery surrounding the murder, it becomes clear that the expectations that one has of this city are not going to be realized. The familiar elements in which the traditional image of the city are rooted are deformed and the suggestions of a folkloric Madrid are systematically undermined. His wanderings take him to Retiro Park, the Plaza de la Cebada, Tirso de Molina's statue, and other places that are supposed to represent the history and memory of the city's inhabitants. However, these representations of unity, continuity, and history in the city are devalued, and as a result they are no longer familiar to Zenón. The Tirso de Molina square, for example, built on the ruins of the convent of La Merced, where the golden age Spanish playwright Tirso de Molina took his vows (Gea Ortigas 1999, 261) is entirely overrun by heroin addicts. This discrepancy between the urban reality lived by Zenón and the suggestions of the true and pure Madrid city is best expressed in the following observation he makes as he approaches Tirso de Molina's statue:

La estatua de Tirso parecía recitar a las palomas, mientras los heroinómanos permanecían semidormidos y algunos entrecruzaban frases de amor. Las palomas andan un poco confundidas porque no distinguen a los poetas pobres de los heroinómanos. Se acercan confiados a éstos, creyendo que son los otros, y en el momento menos pensado se llevan un zapatillazo que las deja alichulas. (43–44)

[Tirso de Molina's statue seemed to be addressing the pigeons while the heroin addicts nodded off and a few exchanged amorous words. The pigeons are rather confused because they cannot tell the difference between poor poets and heroin addicts. They confidently approach the latter mistaking them for the former, and when they least expect it they get a wing-breaking kick.]

The fundamental identity of the city, which one expects to find reflected in its monuments, landmarks, and traditions, is found to be wanting here; like the pigeons, Zenón is seen in this novel to be confused, too, because the events taking place around him do not correspond to his expectations.

In other instances, his bewilderment is shown in his observation of the disjunction between the city and its inhabitants. Zenón's ironic eye captures this exchange between a father and a son in Retiro Park:

> Junto al estanque había un padre de familia con un niño de unos seis años. "¡Mira qué lago!", dijo el padre refiriéndose al estanque. En la orilla se erguía un cisne negro sostenido por una sola pata. El hijo, al verlo, dando muestra del instinto poético de los niños, exclamó: "¡Qué paloma más grande!" El padre, vuelto hacia el cisne, dijo: "¡Vaya pato!", volviendo a manifestar su zafiedad. (65–66)

> [Next to the pond there stood a family man and a kid of about six. "Look, what a lake!" said the father referring to the pond. There was a black swan standing on only one leg at the edge. When the boy saw this he exclaimed, with that poetic instinct typical of kids: "What a huge pigeon!" The father, turned toward the swan, said: "Heck of a duck!", showing his uncouthness once again.]

The son and the father above are, in Zenón's opinion, like the people who

> piensa que en el Retiro sólo hay tías piernonas . . . Cuando pasan ante la estatua del ángel caído dicen "pobre ángel, lo atrapa una serpiente" ¡Ignoran que él es la serpiente porque él es Satanás! (66)

> [think that the Retiro is all girls with nice legs . . . When they go by the statue of the fallen angel, they say "poor angel; he has been caught by a serpent." They don't know that *he* is the serpent because he is Satan.] (Italics mine)

In other words, neither the father nor the son is successful in understanding the world they perceive around them. To the father, the Retiro pond is a lake, while the young son sees one of its many black swans and calls it a pigeon. At that, the father, who appears to know no better, exclaims, "Heck of a duck"! Their ignorance regarding what should be familiar emblems of their city is symptomatic of the breakdown in continuity between past and present embodied in the city. This breakdown in turn suggests a disassociation between the self and its surroundings, a symptom from which Zenón himself appears to be suffering. Furthermore, since the folkloric image of the city represents the traditions and the values of the community, its destruction is equivalent to the disintegration of the social fiber of the community on the one hand, and on the other, the dismantling of its values. In *De Madrid al cielo* the veneer of the traditional city is eroded to reveal the underbelly of Madrid where unemployment, social injustice and urban crime such as prostitution and drug abuse abound. This is the urban context of the film noir genre on which Grasa's novel is modeled.

Zenón manages to solve the crime in the end; however, the solution of the mystery surrounding the crime loses its value because the crime is only a pretext for communicating a deeper existential problem, which remains even after the crime has been solved. The revelation of who the murderer is, his friend Chule, is reminiscent of the ending of *Double Indemnity* when, back in the insurance office where we first meet him, Walter Neff completes the confession he had been dictating for his coworker and friend Keyes. Neff says to him, "You know why you couldn't figure this one, Keyes? . . . 'Cause the guy you were looking for was too close, right across the desk from you." As Keyes notes in his response to this, Neff was not only spatially close to him but also affectively so, and this makes the crime all the more absurd and its resolution even less satisfying from Keyes's point of view.

Similarly, for Zenón, the absurdity of the crime, the senseless murder of a young girl in his bed by a close friend of his, resonates with the absurdity of his existence and confirms his deepest anxieties: the crisis of the masculine identity due to the loss of the prestigious position hitherto accorded to the male subject; his anguish over a world gone all wrong is reflected in the failure of his own communist values and his own failure as an individual and in a city that has lost its character. While returning from the police station where he had gone to report his friend, he buys an expensive guitar. He had previously sold the truck with which he worked as a ragman. With these two acts Zenón marks a symbolic return to the beginning and evokes his film noir model who always returns to the point of departure—his office or apartment—once the crime has been solved. However, Zenón makes the disillusion symbolized by the return to the beginning even clearer when upon leaving the shop he suddenly stops and declares, "ni un paso más" (that's it; not another step) (136), then grabs the guitar with both hands and brings it crashing down against a tree on Santa Isabel Street.

Through this last, apparently inexplicable act, he eloquently expresses his resignation in the face of an existence that from his point of view is entirely meaningless. The murder of a young defenseless woman by his closest friend destroys the last vestiges of confidence that Zenón has in himself and in other men; it reveals the underworld of crime, violence, and the disintegration of the social fabric, and it therefore underlines the failure of his sociopolitical ideals; it reveals the paradoxes hidden in an environment that is unknowable to him because it is missing its fundamental referents. Given these circumstances, Zenón bears the image of the vulnerable protagonist of the film noir subjected to pressures over which he has no control. His reaction after solving the crime reveals the existential helplessness of the noir characters on whom he is modeled.

Ismael Grasa's rendition of film noir motifs in *De Madrid al cielo* allows him to reveal the material and the psychological situation of a character in an urban setting that has been subjected to the socioeconomic transformations associated with 1990s Madrid. The transformations that impact on Gabriela Bustelo's central characters' sense of self, on the other hand, are of a technological nature. They are the outcome of the proliferation of the electronic and audiovisual gadgets that signaled 1990s Spain's integration into the information technology age. In *Veo veo,* therefore, the detective story serves to reveal the vulnerability of the people who inhabit an urban setting that is evidently modified by electronic and audiovisual systems.

Unlike the Madrid in Grasa's novel, the Spanish capital in Gabriela Bustelo's *Veo veo* is not described as a clearly defined space with identifiable localized points of reference. Whereas Grasa's novel is set in a city with certain familiar, albeit transformed signs, the urban landscape in Bustelo's lacks the unique signs with which it might be identified. This is owed to the fact that the monuments and streets that usually characterize cities have been replaced by electronic communication networks. In this novel, Bustelo illustrates how the implosion of technology in the urban environment has brought about changes in the nature of urban space and in the relationship between the subject and that space.

In *Veo veo*, the boundaries between private and public space, for example, are challenged by television broadcasting, telephones, answering machines, and video cameras. A whole world of virtual characters created by the cinema screen invade the subject's private spaces, while a network of high-speed transportation prevents it from coming into intimate contact with real fellow inhabitants of the city. Within this space Bustelo's protagonist, a young screenplay writer, perceives her unstable sense of self as an illogical sensation of being the victim of constant voyeurism. This prompts her to hire a detective who in turn relies on the same intrusive communication technology, rather than clues gathered by walking the streets, to attempt to solve the mystery.

The term "non-place" suggested by Marc Augé appears to be an adequate description for the urban context in Bustelo's novel.[5] For this sociologist, technology today has contributed to the creation of an excess of spaces that he calls "non-places." By this term he means "a space which cannot be defined as relational or historical or concerned with identity" (1995, 77–78). "Place," as opposed to "non-place," is identified with monuments, history, and human interaction. "Non-place" on the other hand, is a location in which the unique identity, history, and organic relationships between subjects are of minimal importance. According to his study, the following italicized expressions and words commonly used in contemporary reality are evidence of the proliferation of "non-places" rather than "places" in the contemporary urban context:

> Thus we can contrast the realities of *transit* (transit camps or passengers in transit) with those of residence or dwelling; the *interchange* (where nobody crosses anyone else's path) with the *crossroads* (where people meet); the *passenger* (defined by his *destination*) with the *traveller* (who strolls along his *route*) . . . [T]he *housing estate* . . . where people do not live together and which is never situated in the centre of anything . . . with the *monument* where people share and commemorate.[6]

According to the above, it is evident that in the "non-place" there is no cohesion between the individual and his or her surroundings and co-inhabitants. Whatever relationship exists between them is a superficial and ephemeral one. The "non-place," therefore, loses its value as a mirror or symbol in which the individual recognizes himself or herself and others.

It is possible to see the setting of *Veo veo* as being any city in the industrialized world rather than as Madrid specifically. This is because most of the events in the novel take place in those types of spaces that Augé describes as "transit points" or "temporary abodes" (1995, 78). They are all independent of other places and other histories; they are places of rapid, superficial, and temporary encounters. For instance, for the most part *Veo veo* takes place in Vania's apartment or in the Madrid bars. Vania's apartment is a transitory space in which she finds that she is detached from her surroundings and other people. It is interesting that the building in which she lives used to be a palace. Now it has been converted into apartments. In other words, it has been transformed from a place steeped in history into a mere site through which people pass without laying down any roots or foundations. Vania lives in her apartment alone, and she does not know her neighbors. Her isolation from others is increased further by the fact that she gets around the city in her car and therefore is not obliged to relate directly with other people.

Similarly Vania's favorite bars correspond to the spaces classified as "non-places" and described by Augé as "a world surrendered to solitary individuality, to the fleeting, the temporary and ephemeral" (1995, 78). It is not to be assumed that these bars are spaces in which patrons form deep and long-standing relationships. Her acquaintances tend to be models, film directors, and advertising agents; that is, people in the entertainment industry who are given only to the experience of the moment. From her complaints about how uninspiring that environment is for her and why she cannot confide in anyone among them, one can tell that in that social milieu people seek immediate and quick gratification through drugs, alcohol, and sex:

El revival de la noche madrileña no me estaba pareciendo para tirar cohetes, la verdad . . . Cada vez me sentía más marciana. No tenía claro en quién podía confiar y en quién no . . . Los noctámbulos no están para películas de suspense. Quieren oír chorradas, reírse, beber y esnifar. De lo demás pasan. (*Veo veo* 1996, 31; future references will be given parenthetically by page number in the text)

[I didn't think this revival of the Madrid night scene was all that exciting . . . I felt more and more like a Martian. I wasn't sure whom I could
trust . . . These night-birds are not interested in suspenseful movies.
They want to hear nonsense, laugh and drink and snort coke. The rest,
they ignore.]

Indeed, the way in which she relates to these solitary acquaintances at the bar requires little commitment and no deep form of
communication, as one can tell from the following confession
about the way in which she chats with a friend: "Valco entró al
trapo y me contó todos los pormenores del affair . . . pero me puse
el piloto automático mientras jugaba al veo-veo con Ben, interca-
lando monosílabos aquí y allá" (Valco reacted and gave me all the
details about the affair . . . but I switched to automatic pilot and
while I played hide and seek with Ben I dropped monosyllables
here and there in the conversation) (61).

The state of "non-place" of the spaces inhabited by Vania is
owed to another reason closely related to technological advancement and the breakdown of the barriers that separate private and
public spaces. In spatial terms, she experiences this transformation as having the sensation of being followed all over the city and
even in her apartment. Indeed, the novel begins with Vania in a
psychiatrist's office trying to find an explanation for that para-
noiac sensation. One day, in desperation, she searches her whole
apartment and discovers, to her alarm, tiny microphones hidden
everywhere. Later, she finds out that a video camera hidden in a
strategic position in her apartment had filmed her in several com-
promising situations. Vania's experiences following these discov-
eries border on the absurd, and at the end of the novel there is the
suggestion that she had dreamed it all. One wonders, therefore, if
the feeling of being watched at all times and the discovery of the
electronic devices are not related to the intrusion of media of communication (film, television, and computers) in the urban experience. This is indeed one more reality of supermodernity according
to Augé, who explains:

We are in an era characterized by the changes in scale . . . [R]apid
means of transportation have brought any capital within a few hours'
travel of any other. And in the privacy of our homes, finally, images of
all sorts, relayed by satellites and caught by aerials that bristle on the
roofs of our remotest hamlets, can give us an instant, sometimes simul-

taneous vision of an event taking place on the other side of the planet. (1995, 31)

One can add that in the supermodern city, private images and information can also be transmitted to the rest of the world at the very moment in which they are produced. No one can escape from the prying eyes of technology in the urban environment.

Bustelo modifies the characteristic investigative activities of the detective in the urban setting to underscore this impact of the communication technology on the city space and her protagonist's vulnerability in that environment. The private detective is a creature of the modern city.[7] The modern urban space, which is crisscrossed by a myriad of historical, social, and cultural references that is recognizable to the community, lends itself to the rational task of investigation undertaken by a detective. Furthermore, the detective is able to carry out his duties and the other characters are able to engage in secretive activities, hidden away from the prying eyes of others, because of the anonymity afforded by the city.[8] In *Veo veo*, however, Madrid is a city whose urban environment can be described as a space "vaciado de su lastre histórico" (divested of its historical burden) (Resina 1997, 167). These conditions affect the process by which Vania's detective attempts to solve the mystery and its outcome.

In fact, in contrast to the conventional detective who is able to solve mysteries by virtue of his knowledge of the urban surroundings and the clues he finds while walking the streets, the one Vania hires simply takes advantage of the intrusion of technology into private spaces to obtain his leads. Detective Peláez depends on a contact who has "acceso a ficheros informáticos secretos donde sale todo, desde las tendencias sexuales hasta las multas de tráfico por ir bebido" (access to secret computer files where he can find anything, from sexual tendencies to drunk-driving fines) (91). Furthermore, Peláez himself has access to all of Vania's personal information, because he in turn hires a "documentalista" (researcher) for whom "no hay sistema informático que le resista" (no computer system is impenetrable) (99). Through his contacts he finds out that Vania is the heir to her family's fortunes. This is information that even Vania herself did not possess. In addition, according to Peláez, all the information that he had compiled on her is also available to some criminals who are planning to use it exploitatively.

Peláez's findings exacerbate rather than assuage Vania's fears. They prove that the anonymity and the individuality that urban dwellers supposedly enjoy in the urban setting of detective fiction have been eliminated by the interpenetration of private and public spaces. Vania had observed irritably that "[s]e suponía que Madrid era una gran capital europea, una ciudad cosmopolita en la que se podía pasar inadvertido, pero yo ya tenía la casa llena de bichos electrónicos y encima me llamaban majaras . . . por teléfono" (Madrid is supposed to be a great European capital, a cosmopolitan city in which one can go about unnoticed, yet my house was already full of electronic bugs and on top of that I was getting phone calls from crazy people) (69). Evidently, that anonymity, and the security that it implies for the subject, cannot be taken for granted in the supermodern city in which the technology explosion has broken down the barriers of isolation.

The encroachment of technology onto Vania's private space is similar to what happens in *The Truman Show*, a film focused on the phenomenon of intrusive electronic voyeurism in contemporary society. In this film the main character lives his whole life without realizing that his everyday existence is being communicated to a world of television viewers. His vital space has been transformed into a fishbowl by means of electronic devices. Vania's own situation is analogous. Her apartment, situated on a street appropriately called "calle del Pez," is like a fishbowl in which, as she says, "lo que ya no se me quitaba de encima era lo del maldito ojo ajeno. Estuviera donde estuviera, en todo momento tenía la impresión de que alguien me miraba" (what I could not get rid of was the damn intrusive eye. Wherever I was, I had the impression that someone was watching me all the time) (90). Of course, *The Truman Show* could not have been the inspiration for Bustelo's novel, as it came out two years after the latter was published. What is clear, however, is that both are anchored in the recognition of the instability of urban spatial boundaries due to the contemporary audiovisual and digital technology explosion.[9]

In this urban space transformed by audiovisual and digital technology, Vania is vulnerable, not only because she loses her anonymity, but also because her individuality diminishes in favor of a shared identity. It is important to note that a separate private space not only provides intimate existence but also contributes to the creation of the unique individual. This is because within the private space the subject is bound to have access to exclusive messages that will contribute to the formation of differentiating identities. Vania does not enjoy this privilege, because she does not have access to an isolated space. She shares her space either at home or in the bars with the public, and with the latter she receives the same images and messages simultaneously through the same media of communication. Vania does not stand out in any way in her environment. She is really one more young woman among a host of others who carry out the same predetermined roles. Her lack of original experiences in this "non-place" is most evident when she realizes that a patient who she meets at a mental institution has had a similar experience to her own: "Además, mis síntomas coincidían casi uno por uno con los del ingeniero del porche. El complot, las pruebas, los espías, las señales, la culpabilidad, el arrebato místico, el escaso interés sexual" (in addition, my symptoms were almost exactly like those of the engineer I had met on the porch. The plot, the tests, the spies, the signs, the guilt, the mystical outburst and the low libido) (173).[10]

With the barriers between private and public space broken down by the media of communication, a world of cinematographic images invades the private space of the subject. This fictitious world replaces the traditional urban reality and it is in that fictitious world that Vania is able to find direction as she confesses: "Poco a poco había ido descubriendo una forma completamente distinta de relacionarse [sic] con lo real. La imagen. Otro mundo en el que la rapidez y el instante concreto eran lo que contaba" (slowly, I had been discovering a completely different way of relating to reality. Image. Another world in which speed and the concrete moment were what counted] (64). Augé provides an explanation for this phenomenon in which the world of visual images is imposed on the concrete experience in the urban context:

[A]ll space consumers thus find themselves caught among the echoes and images of a sort of cosmology which . . . is objectively universal, and at the same time familiar and prestigious. This has at least two results. On the one hand, these images tend to make a system; they outline a world of consumption that every individual can make his own because it buttonholes him incessantly . . . On the other hand, like all cosmologies, this new cosmology produces effects of recognition. (1995, 106)

In the same way, as certain brand names create immediately recognizable and understandable signs in the globalized world of supermodernity, cinema and television also engender a new cosmology with recognizable reference signs. Vania obviously lives and works in that cosmology. Since she is a screenplay writer and works in film, her vision is mediated through the world of images.

From the first step that she takes to deal with the issue of the people following her, she traps the reader into a world of television and movie characters. This situation heightens the mystery, as it is then not clear if she is experiencing in reality what she is going through. When she goes to visit the psychiatrist, a man who, according to her, looked like Mickey Rourke leads her into a room with white pine furnishing and cushions (10). She had expected to see "una especie de vejete judío con barba, firme y paternal a la vez" (some old bearded Jewish guy who was firm yet fatherly) who had "muebles de caoba y butacas de esas de cuero que se amoldan a la nalga" (mahogany furniture and those leather armchairs that fit the shape of the buttocks) (ibid.). Furthermore, that psychiatrist asks her questions "como hacen siempre los psiquiatras en las películas" (like the psychiatrists in the films always do), and she in turn answers "en la misma línea" (in the same way) (ibid.).

Thus, in a moment of confusion, when it is not clear at all if all her experience has been real or just a hallucination, she says:

Clic. Se me volvió a encender la cámara de cine mental. Yo era la pobre víctima descerebrada que justo intenta convencer de su inocencia al Terrible Doctor Flunkenstein, que tiene un fichero de lo más completo sobre mi conducta social, familiar, sexual, profesional . . . Intenté saltar al otro lado de la pantalla, volver al patio de butacas, ver todo aquello simplemente como el momento más emocionante de la película, pero por primera vez no lo conseguí. (162)

[Click. The imaginary film camera goes off in my head again. I was the poor, foolish victim just trying to prove her innocence to the Terrible Dr. Flunkenstein who has the most complete file on my social and family life and on my sexual and professional behavior . . . I tried to jump to the other side of the screen, return to the seats, simply see all that as the most exciting moment in the movie; but for the first time I couldn't.]

Vania has transferred all her experience to the world of the movie screen. She and her experiences have abandoned the real streets in order to inhabit the uncertain world of film and television. The subject, as well as her environment and her experiences in these circumstances, lose their stability and tangibility and oscillate precariously between the real world and the virtual world. Her experience confirms Michael Dear's observation that

> [O]ur geographies have radically shifted: from sidewalk into traffic; from car to screen; from arcade to inside your head; from stasis to speed. Your postmodern, mobile/virtual gaze dwells in a phantasmagoria of the interior, a hyper-real society of spectacle . . . The conflation between material and virtual worlds, between spaces of the screen and spaces of the street, is part of the postmodern condition that we are only now confronting. (2000, 210)

Although *Veo veo* is developed along the plotlines of detective fiction, it does not have a closed ending. Vania concludes that her adventures had been "un delirio, una alucinación óptica" (a delirium, an optical hallucination) (178). She therefore leaves a big question mark on the validity of her very existence. This confusion between the real and the imagined is not surprising, because Vania's experiences develop in an environment in which there has been a breakdown of the barriers that are supposed to separate space into concrete units. The communication media opens the private domain out to public interference, and this leaves her in the absurd situation in which material walls offer no protection or intimacy. At the same time, however, the communication media provides Vania with a wider world of experiences and relationships that replace those of the concrete world. Her experiences are thus astride two spaces: the concrete one that is her apartment, the bars and the streets of Madrid, on one hand, and that of the communication media, on the other, with the latter taking precedence over the former.

Neither Grasa nor Bustelo can claim that urban spaces are the embodiment of their characters' being. Rather, both authors have managed to bring out through the detective genre the obstacles to their characters' sense of security, their knowledge of themselves and of others and their general sense of stability in the cities in which they dwell. In Grasa's novel these impediments are clearly rooted in the socioeconomic realities affecting his protagonist. In Bustelo's case, it is the impact of audiovisual and digital technology on the city that affects her protagonist's existential certainty.

3

Powerless Subjects in Credit Card Democracies: Belén Gopegui in *La conquista del aire* and *Lo real*

THE FOUR NOVELS STUDIED SO FAR ARE ALL CHARACTERIZED BY AN engagement with popular cultural discourse. *Historias del Kronen* and *La pistola de mi hermano* are self-consciously rooted in popular audiovisual entertainment and the consumer culture of the nineties. *De madrid al cielo* and *Veo veo* borrow their characters and their environment from detective fiction and film. It appears, then, that Gopegui's "serious" fiction is out of place in this study. Furthermore, Gopegui has been known to dismiss novels such as the above as products of a consumer culture that are not unlike other entertainment media like television.[1] In addition, Belén Gopegui's novels do not revolve around the common urban issues of drugs, sex, and violence with which many other Generation X novelists are often associated. In reality, however, Gopegui's novels reflect the same generational ontological concerns as do the four novels dealt with in the previous chapters. Gopegui articulates a similar concern with the diminishing of the subject's identity in the postcapitalist, media-dominated setting of 1990s Spain in a political discourse that positions agency against economic authoritarianism.

La conquista del aire and *Lo real* focus on characters who have grown up in democratic Spain but whose autonomy appears to be compromised because of the normative socioeconomic practices associated with the 1990s. Gopegui questions the power of her characters to define themselves and to effect change in an environment in which political totalitarianism has been eliminated only to be replaced by the tyranny of the market and the values associated with it. Through dates and historical references Gopegui clearly

71

sets her novels in the first few years of the nineties. This is the period in which Spanish modernity and prosperity were celebrated through spectacles such as the Olympic Games and the Universal Exposition in Sevilla. Gopegui's novels, however, stand out as an alternative version of the official narrative of freedom, democracy, and prosperity communicated through those nineties celebrations.

The 1992 Olympic Games in Barcelona, the Universal Exposition in Sevilla, and the celebration of the quincentenary of Columbus's voyage of "discovery" did more than serve as symbols of Spain's transformation into a modern, democratic Western nation. The 400,000-million peseta (Richardson 2001, 44) face-lift bestowed on Barcelona and the spectacular opening of the Games, for example, combined to reflect not only technological advancement in one of the most important Spanish cities but also served as a representation of the achievement of a balance between regional uniqueness, national pride, and European affluence. A related spirit of openness to diversity and the acceptance of the other were the hallmarks of Expo '92. In this milestone celebration Spain appeared to make amends for the atrocities of its colonial and imperial past by acknowledging its Arab heritage through the designs of Spanish pavilions and the exhibition of Moorish art in one of the major exhibitions of the event "Arte y cultura en torno a 1492" (Art and Culture about 1492) (Morgan, 2000, 62). Similarly, the assertion of Castilian hegemony was replaced by a show of diversity in the regional pavilions. Although the very celebration of Columbus's arrival in the Americas smacked of imperialistic and colonial sentiments, it provided the forum to reassess the nature and consequences of the European encounter with transatlantic indigenous populations. Furthermore, as Bill Richardson has observed, the events of the celebration provided the stage for reaching out to Jewish cultures through the exhibition of Jewish art in the exposition "La vida judía en Sefarad" (Sephardic Jewish Life), which displayed "artefacts relating to the lives of Jews who had been expelled from Spain in 1492 and who had migrated to Central and Eastern Europe" (Richardson 2001, 45). To the thousands of viewers who watched the Olympic Games as well as to the Spanish people who thronged to the Expo '92 pavilions and cultural sites that celebrated the quincentenary of Columbus's voyage, there was no doubt that Spain had definitively shed its image of the "poor cousin" imposed upon it by decades of autarkic, isolationist, xenophobic, and insular domestic, foreign, and economic policies upheld in the name of a mythic national identity. The events of 1992 were statements designed to articulate in no uncertain terms the opening up and modernization of Spain (Morgan 2000, 58).

These statements were further driven home by the symbolism in the launching of Spain's first communications satellite, Hispasat. This satellite, billed as the "tercer gran acontecimiento del 92" (the third greatest event in '92) was built in record time (thirty-three months) to coincide with the significant year.[2] It had the capacity to "transmitir comunicaciones de todo tipo, incluidos canales de televisión directa que se podrán recibir en España con antenas muy pequeñas, de unos 40 centímetros de diámetro" (transmit all kinds of communications, including television channels that will be able to be received in Spain with very small antennas of about 40cms in diameter).[3] The 1992 celebrations were no doubt an eloquent statement that Spain had abandoned its Middle Ages values and boarded the train of progress to catch up with fellow Europeans.

The preceding observations, however, represent only one level of the meaning of these events that also constitute the official narratives of contemporary Spain's modernity and affluence. The second and less evident level of meaning points to an equally significant step in Spain's transformation at the end of the twentieth century. It reveals in this official story the culmination of Spain's deviation from the tenets of social democracy to fully embrace those of neoliberalism. If the first level of interpretation tells of the displacement of political authoritarianism, the second is an enunciation of its replacement with the authority of the economy rather than with the privileging of social participation as would have been expected. For, while the then-mayor of Barcelona, Pasquall Maragall, proclaimed in 1992 that "we have proudly recovered a plural Hispanic identity" (quoted in Morgan 2000, 64), the voices of dissent calling for social reforms that conflicted with the quest for capital to finance the 1992 celebrations were, in the main, ignored. Social participation in the democratic Spain of the 1990s was submitted to the rules of economic growth. Indeed, it has been suggested that political liberalization in Spain—which began even under Franco—was promoted for its contribution to capital growth. In the 1992 celebrations Spain made a show of its new globally acceptable image of a nation open to diversity over the assertion of authoritarian national values. The latter alternative, in the context of contemporary global politics and economics, was nothing but an impediment to capital mobility and economic growth. Indeed, by 1992 it was evident that political totalitarianism had been eroded forever and the specter of Francoism was completely exorcised. At the same time it was evident that the empowerment of the people promised by the socialist government was being undermined by the power of capital. It is this reality behind the official version of Spain's progress in the nineties that informs Belén Gopegui's engagement with the human condition in her novels *La conquista del aire* and *Lo real.*

Gopegui's provision of precise dates and references to events in both novels enables the reader to situate them in a particular historical context. *La conquista del aire,* for example, begins in 1994, on Tuesday, October 11, (*La conquista* 1998, 17; future references will be given parenthetically by page number in the text) the day one of the three central characters, Carlos, asks for a loan from the other two, his friends. It ends "[e]n la madrugada del 26 de noviembre de 1996" (in the early morning of November 26, 1996) (341). The events in the novel take place in a two-year period in the midnineties, a time in which the Spanish society as a whole, according to social historians, was undergoing an existential crisis as a result of the contradictions in its system of government. Luis Palacios Bañuelos states, on the eve of the year 1994, that:

No es posible a la hora de encararnos con el nuevo año 1994 evadirnos de la crisis que nos rodea. Crisis que supera lo económico. Estamos también ante una nueva crisis, o tal vez cambio, de valores cuestionándose toda una cosmovisión. (2001, 337)

[As we are about to face this new year, 1994, we cannot avoid the crisis that surrounds us. This crisis goes beyond the economic. We are also facing a new crisis or perhaps a change of values that questions a whole worldview.]

The crisis to which Palacios Bañuelos refers is aggravated by the people's loss of faith in the Socialist Party (PSOE), which, after thirteen years in government, subsequently lost the 1996 elections to the opposition, the conservative Partido Popular. In its final years in power, the PSOE had managed to sow seeds of doubt and despair in the minds of the population with respect to the value and meaning of Spain's relatively young democracy as a result of its socio-economic policies and the corruption scandals that plagued the party.

In his assessment of Spain in that period, historian Santos Juliá also explains that "la gran mayoría de los ciudadanos compartían valores democráticos" (the vast majority of the citizens shared democratic values); for them the period of democracy that began with great expectations in the seventies had by the nineties left the democratically minded with a feeling of great frustration (1999, 278–79). Indeed, some of the characters in *La conquista del aire* express similar sentiments of frustration, especially with the PSOE's ideological ambiguity. It was not clear to some of them that "la derecha" (the right) referred only to the Partido Popular, because, as Marta, one of the friends, explains, "la derecha, bajo distintos nombres, ha impuesto su modelo de forma global" (the Right, under the guise of various names, has imposed its model globally) (199). Her observation is no doubt directed at the general pursuit by the Spanish government of the time, and by other social democratic European countries, of economic policies once associated with the political right. Gopegui's characters give expression to the betrayal felt by the Left as a result of the PSOE's neoliberal economic policies, which compromised the traditional socialist principles. The economic boom that Spain experienced in the eighties as well as its economic and political modernization hailed both at home and abroad in the three spectacular celebrations, for example, soon proved to have been attained at a price that was especially dear to the predominantly working-class supporters of the Socialist Party, as Palacios Bañuelos observes in 1993: "Pero si tuviéramos que elegir una sola palabra como definitoria del verano del 93 sin duda acudiríamos a la palabra crisis. Crisis económica antes y más que nada. Y sus consecuencias: intranquilidad, inseguridad, malestar social y, sobre todo, paro" (but if we had to choose a single word that defined the summer of '93, we would undoubtedly choose the word crisis. Economic crisis first and foremost. And its consequences: worry, insecurity, social unease and above all unemployment) (2001, 328).

In addition, political scandal surrounding the PSOE contributed further to destabilize public faith in such values as civic responsibility and the rule of law hitherto championed by the party. Fernando Jiménez Sánchez accurately summarizes the irony of a Socialist Party blatantly engaged in corruption and its effect on the Spanish psyche with reference to the Juan Guerra scandal, in particular:

> En síntesis, los hechos que van a dar lugar al escándalo son los siguientes: un socialista enriquecido (lo que no sólo irá contra los valores defendidos por el ala izquierda del partido, sino por el propio líder del mismo); que además se ha hecho rico partiendo de la nada merced a negocios en los que aparece siempre la mano de alguna Administración pública con concesiones, recalificaciones, etcétera. (1995, 170).

> [In short, the facts that are going to cause the scandal are as follows: a socialist who got rich (which violated not only the values held by the left wing of the party but also those held by the leader himself); and who, moreover, has gone from rags to riches thanks to deals in which there is always some public Administration involvement with concessions, rezoning, etc.]

To Francisco Romero Salvadó, therefore, "[u]nder the leadership of Felipe González and Alfonso Guerra, the PSOE was transformed beyond recognition . . . The old working-class party was replaced by a group of middle-class professionals mostly interested in preserving their lucrative jobs. Lacking any serious political challenge, the government began to identify itself with the state" (1999, 181).

This is the context in which one must read Marta's observation that the PSOE, "han traficado con los valores de la izquierda. Han corrompido las palabras, el significado de la política" (have trafficked with the values of the Left. They have corrupted words, the meaning of politics) (199). She echoes the sentiments of the Spanish population captured in a 1992 opinion poll carried out by the Centro de Investigaciones Sociológicas. In this survey in which 55 percent of those polled thought that their government's economic policies were either "poco adecuada" (inadequate) or "nada adecuada" (not at all adequate), 39 percent of the people agreed with the sentence "la política económica del Gobierno es demasiado conservadora, impropia de un gobierno socialista" (the economic policy of the Government is too conservative, inappropriate for a socialist government) as opposed to the 15 percent who agreed that it was "propia de un gobierno socialista" (appropriate for a socialist government) and the 20 percent who considered it "ade-cuada a las circunstancias" (apropriate under the circumstances).[4]

The sociohistorical context in which *La conquista del aire* and *Lo real* are set, then, is what Santos Sanz Villanueva, in his review of the former, calls "el entorno del puro pragmatismo de la dicta-dura del mercado" (the environment of pure pragmatism of the dictatorship of the market) (1998). This is the same context that Gopegui disparagingly describes elsewhere as the "democracia de tarjeta de crédito" (credit card democracy) (2001a). It is no won-der then that Gopegui chooses to use money as the point of depar-ture and the driving force behind the narrative of *La conquista del aire*, and underlines its corrupting influence and ubiquitous na-ture in all levels of human activities and relationships in *Lo real*. If for the preceding generation of novelists the source of conflict with their environment was political totalitarianism, for Gopegui and her generation, the power against which they write has shifted from the political to the economic sphere. As Alain Touraine sug-gests in "Social Transformations of the Twentieth Century" (1998), in today's democracies the throne continues to be in place. What has changed is the entity that occupies it. That entity that continues to undermine agency within contemporary democracies is economic in nature.

In this sense then, there is an element of continuity between the totalitarian context that inspired previous anti-Francoist fiction in the post–civil war era and that of these two novels by Gopegui. This continuity is suggested in *Lo real*, as the author herself pointed out during the Barcelona launching of the novel. There she explained that "[h]e querido poner la historia del padre, una historia de corrupción durante el franquismo, porque creo que hubo una cierta continuidad entre el franquismo y lo que vino des-pués" (I wanted to include the father's story, a story about corrup-tion during Francoism, because I believe that there was a certain continuity between Francoism and what came afterward).[5] She was referring to the main life experience that colors the protago-nist Edmundo's worldview and serves as the point of reference in his vital choices. It is a story of corruption in which his father, an employee of MATESA, a textile machinery factory, was found guilty for his role in a corruption scandal in which the Opus Dei was implicated.[6] Edmundo considered his father, sentenced to twenty months' imprisonment for his part in the crime, a mere scapegoat in a trial in which "habían pagado los pequeños pecadores por los grandes" (the small-time sinners had paid on behalf of the big-time ones) (*Lo real* 2000, 20; future references will be given parenthetically by page number in the text). In his opinion, the more powerful people continued to wield their authority in the status quo even after 1975, while rewarding their scapegoat with certain favours. Among these favors was Edmundo's own admission into the School of Journalism at the University of Navarra and his acceptance into an Opus Dei–run *colegio mayor* (university residence) there. He was both a victim and a beneficiary of the corruption and nepotism rife in the Franco regime.

It is suggested in *Lo real* that the end of Francoism did not diminish the power of the Francoists. Edmundo himself observes as much when by 1977 he notes that he had not experienced that "estallido" (explosion) (43) that he had expected following the death of Franco. As the narrator puts it "(l)a democracia se encontraba a la vuelta de la esquina y las familias de los compañeros de clase de Edmundo comprendían que no iban a perder el poder aunque quizá sí tuvieran que compartirlo" (democracy was just around the corner and the families of Edmundo's friends understood that they were not going to lose power even though perhaps they were going to have to share it) (43–44). Indeed, the truly powerful in the regime did not really lose their power in the transition. Continuity between the past and the present is evident in the unwavering prestige and privilege enjoyed by the Maldonado family, whose oldest son, Fernando, is a friend and contemporary of Edmundo's. This upper-middle-class family continued to enjoy the same privileges as they had in the Franco regime. What is more, in the post-Franco era, the professional position of Fernando and Edmundo reflected the same social inequality that had always existed between them. In fact, Fernando was well placed professionally because of his family's position, and Edmundo on occasion had to rely on his friend's contacts to fulfill his own professional ambitions.

The novel abounds with allusions to similar expressions of disappointments of people who had not experienced that "estallido" (explosion) that would have brought about a radical break with the past. The most evident of these allusions is the story of the narrator herself, a woman who rebelled against traditional gender roles in her youth. As a young woman she did not see herself simply as the "mestiza" but rather as the "pistolero" (gunman) himself in a Western (250), shooting at the laws that sought to impose themselves on her will. Today, at fifty, she does not consider that she and other women have won the right to assert themselves. On the contrary, she believes that "[l]as mujeres estábamos para refrendar un mundo ya firmado" (we women were there to ratify an already signed world) (266); their efforts have served to endorse, not radically change, the existing reality. In her opinion what they have achieved is still considered the exception to the rule rather than the norm. Comparing herself in this regard to her husband, she says:

> quise decirle a Blas: . . . ¿No ves cómo todo lo que consigo está manchado de polvo, sudor, es fruto de saqueo, concesión de los señores de la guerra y cómo, por el contrario, lo que consigues tú te pertenece, te cae tan natural como un buen traje a quien pueda ponérselo y a mí me queda siempre un poco grande, un poco corto o ancho como ropa prestada? (266)

> [I wanted to say to Blas: . . . Don't you see how everything that I achieve is already stained with dust, sweat, is the fruit of plunder, the concession of the lords of war; and how what you achieve, on the other hand, belongs to you, suits you as naturally as a good suit, which for me is always a little too big, a little too short or too wide, like borrowed clothes?]

Gopegui's dismissal of the transition period as representing a real break between the Francoist regime and the so-called democratic era has also been expressed by many sociologists and political scientists as well. Vicenç Navarro, for example, has observed that Francoism was not defeated. For him, Francoism "[s]e fue transformando, adaptándose al hecho democrático" (progressively changed and adapted itself to the fact of democracy) (2002, 186) and that the post-Francoist values of the transition began under Franco himself as a necessity to make Spain acceptable to the European Economic Community. What is more, the architects of the transition, in his opinion, were dominated by conservative values, as the Left had been weakened by the many years of dictatorship. The control wielded by conservative forces in the transition resulted, according to Navarro, in the culture of amnesia in post-Franco Spain. Others have noted that the left was obliged to compromise its values during the Transition to avoid the sort of extreme ideological and cultural positions that resulted in the civil war.

It is further suggested in Gopegui's novels that the continuity between the post-Franco era and the dictatorship itself is not only a political one. It has to do, more importantly, with similarities in value systems. That the agency of the individual continues to be undermined even after Franco cannot be attributed simply to a betrayal on the part of the Left, to a compromise between the major players, or to the continued presence of Francoist elements in the transition government. Both periods are viewed in Gopegui's fiction as totalitarian, to the extent that the predominant values in both systems operate by undermining individuality and agency in one way or another. Francoism is generally condemned for this reason while the post-Franco period is often unreservedly celebrated for empowering the individual. The simplification is not lost on Gopegui.

In totalitarian Spain under Franco, the conflict between the subject and the center of authority was sociopolitical in nature. The imposition of a one-party state on the Spanish population, the hegemony of the Church, the oligarchy of the landowning elite, and the suppression of regionalism were all meant to consolidate national unity and integrity. In response, subject construction during this period involved a process of the production of social mechanisms to counteract state "appropriation of individuation" (Touraine 1998, 170). Since the state's power was aimed at controlling socially or politically determined groups—feminists, communists, nationalists, and other minority groups—, the resistance against it or, in other words, the mechanisms of self-actualization to combat the hegemony of the state, was produced from the perspective of collective sociopolitical identities anchored in stable and secure locations of collective identification. The cultural representation of this process can be found in the proliferation of literary and audiovisual works that reaffirmed social or sexual identities in the immediate post-Franco period.

The replacement of state hegemony with economic control, however, profoundly changes the relationship between the subject and the source of power, because the power of capital itself, as opposed to that of the state, is not concentrated in one identifiable location. Whereas in the totalitarian era in Spain the "throne" or center was occupied by the state and its representative institutions—the Church, the big banks, and the landowning elite—today it is occupied by capital, and according to Manuel Castells's analysis of the postindustrial societies, we cannot expect capital to be solely in the hands of capitalist firms and corporate media. It is, according to his study, "diffused in global networks of wealth, power, information, and images, which circulate and transmute in a system of variable geometry and dematerialized geography" (1997, 359). Touraine, whom Castells quotes in an epigraph in *The Power of Identity*, also says as much: "Power used to be in the hands of princes, oligarchies, and ruling elites; it was defined as the capacity to impose one's will on others, modifying their behavior. This image of power does not fit our reality any longer. Power is everywhere and nowhere: it is in mass production, in financial flows, in lifestyles, in the hospital, in the school, in television, in images, in messages, in technologies" (quoted in Castells 1997, 309).

The shift in the sites of power as described by Castells and Touraine may be used to describe the evolution of Spanish political, social, and economic structure in the last four decades of the twentieth century. The transition from the Francoist dictatorship to a socialist government that increasingly adopted neoliberal democratic policies had transferred power, by the nineties, from the state, not to the people, as left-wing militants might have expected, but rather to diffused sites in the globalized capitalist culture of commodity production and consumption. As Spain made the transition from Francoist autarky to a market economy, so too did power shift from state supervision and control to remote sites in New York, London, and Brussels, for example, as changes in key areas of development such as communication media and capital flow show. In Spain broadcast media, for example, has evolved from being solely controlled by the state-owned Radiotelevisión Española (RTVE). This organization, according to Richard Maxwell, was "tightly controlled by the dictatorship, more so than any other medium" and was "Franco's vision and voice" (1995, 5 and 11). However, since the early eighties, RTVE has been sharing its audience with regional broadcasters in the Basque country and in Cataluña, as well as with private media corporations. In the process power may have been wrested from the state, but it still exists dispersed in the interests of banks, large multinational companies, and within sectors of the media industry, whose decisions are not even made on Spanish soil and has nothing to do with Spanish identity.

On one level, the diffusion of the sites of power implies that to assert itself the subject has to negotiate its identity, not with one centralized source of power, but with all the diverse and diffuse agents who control capital flow. On another and more important level, the shift in the sites of power undermines the subject because it makes its resistance to domination difficult. This is because in its diffuse state, power permeates unsuspecting areas of society to such a degree that even the subject itself risks being absorbed by the former. Consequently, the subject is displaced from its position of conflict with the site of power and transformed into a participant of its own domination.

Such is the case of the protagonists in *La conquista del aire* who find themselves unable to uphold their identity as autonomous individuals pitched against a hostile environment in the current mercantile environment. Marta Timoner, Santiago Álvarez, and Carlos Maceda are young Marxists who spent their university years on one side of the battle lines drawn between them (communists and sympathizers of pro-worker movements, as well as spokespeople of the underrepresented in society) and the visible determinants of identity in Francoist Spain (the state, the Church, and other state-sanctioned institutions). Unfortunately they anachronistically continue to define themselves in terms of their resistance to power concentrated in the state and its institutions. Prior to Marta and Santiago lending money to Carlos, the three friends had envisaged themselves as subjects possessing a unified, self-knowing identity alienated from a hostile and unjust environment.

As young Marxists, Carlos, Santiago, and Marta claimed a separation from predetermined "irrational" social associations. Marta, one of two children of wealthy parents, liked to think that her actions and her relationship to society were determined less by pre-established circumstances than by her chosen ideological position. Marta chose to belong to what her husband disdainfully referred to as "la pandilla" (the gang), that is, to "el grupo de amigos que opone sus propias reglas a las reglas de un mundo exterior y hostil" (the group of friends who resisted the rules of the hostile outside world with their own rules) (35). Whether she chose to associate with young Marxists or Catholics, Marta appeared to be making every effort to avoid being grouped with the "grupo de los que tienen" (group of haves) (50); that is, to the social group to which she belonged by reason of birth. For all her effort Santiago still thought that "Marta era menos Marta de lo que Santiago era Santiago, porque Marta era casi todo herencia y [él se] había construido solo" (Marta was less Marta than Santiago was Santiago, because Marta was almost all inheritance and he had made himself) (291–92).

Santiago may be partly right as, unlike Marta, he is more typical of the "newer post-industrial middle classes" (Lash 1990, 20). Considering his humble beginnings in Murcia, it is evident that his position now as a university professor cannot be traced back to an established middle class. In his opinion, had his background been a determinant of his destiny, he would have ended up taking over his father's bar when the latter died, regardless of his own academic achievements. Hence, his confident but highly debatable proclamation that "Yo soy . . . mi propia providencia" (I am . . . my own providence) (334). Like the other two, Carlos also carved out an identity that separated him from his background and placed him within a group of his choice. He shared with his chosen group the laudable goal of working for the common social good. This vital objective is also evident in his reasons for setting up his own company:

> Haría una empresa digna, suya. Tendría algo suyo y, por lo tanto, en cierto modo autónomo, un sitio donde librarse de la arbitrariedad. Allí nadie podría trasladarle, utilizarle, nadie se consideraría con derecho a disponer de su energía . . . Desde su empresa intentaría preservar un recinto civilizado en la selva del capital. (139)

> [He would create his own worthy company. He would have something of his own and, therefore, autonomous in a certain way; a place where he would be free of arbitrariness. There, no one would be able to transfer him or use him. No one would think they had the right to own his energy . . . From his company he would try to preserve a civilized spot in the jungle of capitalism.]

From this position they felt confident to see in themselves the possibility for change, propelled by a vision best articulated by Santiago Álvarez as "voluntarismo pequeñoburgués o la creencia en el mérito propio, en el esfuerzo individual como instrumento para corregir las injusticias de la lucha de clases" (that petit bourgeois belief in willpower or self-worth, in the virtue of individual effort as a means of correcting the injustices in the class struggle) (63). This vision appears to be an anachronistic echo of modernist grand narratives: a belief in universal humanism, in the assumption of the leadership of the middle class in spearheading the move toward a more rational organization of a just society as the ultimate sign of progress. This vision is what prompts Santiago, even toward the end of the novel when he has reasons to doubt the validity of his social beliefs, to proclaim to his girlfriend Leticia that "No, Leticia, no creo en la providencia. Yo soy . . . mi propia providencia" (No, Leticia, I don't believe in providence. I am . . . my own providence) (334). It is the same vision that motivates all three friends to embrace socialism from the comfort of their middle-class lives. This belief is the driving force that motivates Carlos to set up his electronic company "Jard," as Marta explains to another friend: "para Carlos la industria era una militancia: no una afición, ni una inversión, ni una necesidad. Era el fruto de un convencimiento partidario: la lucha por lo que debe ser se decide en relación a lo que es y, por lo tanto, producir lo que es forma parte de la lucha" (for Carlos, being in the industrial sector was a militant act: not a hobby, nor an investment, nor a necessity. It was the result of a partisan persuasion: the struggle for what he should be is determined in relation to what he is and therefore producing what he is forms part of the struggle) (59).

This position is, however, unrealistic in their current environment as it presupposes that the subjects adopting it possess an independent, stable, and coherent identity that should enable them to stand in opposition to a similarly absolute, if disconcerting, reality. In the current socioeconomic order, however, in which deregulation and liberalization have changed not only the object of their resistance but also its location, such a position is untenable. The three are weakened in their positions of opposition by their failure to realize that they are not external to the source of power that they confront but that, rather, they are engulfed at various levels of their lives by it and have thus become unwilling participants in their domination. This explains the contradictions in their assumptions and beliefs and in their relationship to the contemporary institutions of power. In other words, within the new order of economic totalitarianism, even their position as individuals opposed to a hostile environment is called into question. They are a part of the system that controls them.

As disaffected individuals, they expected to be able to challenge society, successfully or unsuccessfully, from a position of self-assuredness as autonomous beings, like the protagonists of social novels set in the mines, factories, or the agricultural industry had always done. However, they are not even like typical youth characters who, because of their circumstances, may view the controllers of established institutions as obstacles to their progress and self-expression. They are not unemployed students or young people doing "Mcjobs" for a living or trying to get a writing or music career off the ground. Gopegui's characters in *La conquista del aire* are college-educated professionals in their thirties who walk the corridors of corporate offices or are in similar positions of authority. Carlos is an engineer/entrepreneur; Marta, a consultant at the Ministry of Transportation; and Santiago, a university history professor. This distribution of professions is relevant to the social significance of the novel as they represent three sectors of the middle class in postindustrial capitalist Spain of the nineties: the business or financial sector, the bureaucracy, and the intellectual class, respectively. In order to understand their conflicts and concerns, it is necessary to distinguish them from "older dominant bourgeois groupings" (Lash 1990, 19) and identify them rather with "the newer post-industrial middle classes with their bases in media, higher education, finance, advertising, merchandising, and international exchanges" (ibid., 20). That is, they are a new breed of middle class born out of the accelerated integration of Spain into the modern European/American economic, social, and cultural arena.

Clearly, Gopegui's characters are thrust into and are a part of the world of liberalized trade and investment and high-tech development supported by a neoliberal democracy. They find themselves in a situation in which their visions of themselves and their relationship to others, built on a certain notion of a coherent unified self, have fallen apart in the new socioeconomic environment. Within this environment, identity based on chosen, rather than inherited, social relationships gives way to one dependant on modes of consumption and lifestyle that are external to the subject's control. This is similar to the process of identity formation described by Dunn as follows: "Whereas in early capitalism the relations of production became a primary determinant of identity, with the growth of consumer society, occupational identifications have slowly weakened relative to the ascendancy of consumption and lifestyle" (1998, 57–58). The problem of identity within *La conquista del aire* is largely owed to the fact that even the differences that the three friends thought set them apart from normative society and that they considered to be self-constructed are in fact consumed differences. Dunn explains that although socially constructed identities may persist they are "subsumed by the role of consumption, which increasingly shapes and conditions the individual's social orientations and relationships" (ibid., 66). This seems to be the case with Marta and her friends as she observes that:

> Ser de izquierdas, entre su gente, se había convertido en un ritual estético. Tanto ella como sus amigos mantenían buenas relaciones con la propiedad, con los pisos de sus padres que un día heredarían . . . Y, no obstante, todos eran de izquierdas, porque leían a ciertos autores, porque se vestían de cierta manera y porque no les sobraba el dinero. (60)

> [Among her people, belonging to the left wing had become a superficial ritual. She and her friends continued to have a good relationship with property, with their parents' apartments, which they would inherit one day . . . Nevertheless, they were all leftists because they read certain authors, because they dressed in a certain way and because they did not have more money than they needed.]

This process of subject formation, where identity hinges on signs and images, Baudrillard explains, "eliminates . . . the specificity of each human being, and substitutes the *differential* form, which can be industrialized and commercialized as a distinguishing sign" (1998, 93). These distinguishing signs, far from being irreducible, are, in Baudrillard's opinion, exchangeable signs and can be purchased. Baudrillard explains that

> Current differences (of clothing, ideology, and even sex) are exchanged within a vast consortium of consumption. This is a socialized exchange of signs. And if everything can be exchanged in this way, in the form of signs, this is not by virtue of some "liberalization" of

mores, but because differences are systematically produced in accordance with an order which integrates them all as identifying signs and, being substitutable one for another, there is no more tension or contradiction between them than there is between high and low or left and right. (ibid.)

That is, if in an attempt to alienate oneself from an imposed set of values one merely adopts a ready-made set of images of identification through the consumption of shared signs, one weakens the supposed individuality and autonomy implied in subject formation and continues to propagate social contradictions rather than eliminate them. This is particularly important in understanding the conflicts experienced by the characters in *La conquista del aire*. It appears that their claim to a self-constructed identity is only an illusion.

Marta's observation, quoted above, is right. Their Marxism is acquired. Their political identity itself is reduced to being determined by what they eat, wear, drink, and drive. As Marxists, their affiliations with the proletariat are determined merely by their consuming habits, as each of them continues to be attached to their essential or predetermined social class. It is easy to pick out the consumer items or objects with which they inscribe their identity. All three, to a very large extent, indulge in what Baudrillard calls "underconsumption" or "inconspicuous consumption" (1999, 90). That is, from the position of privilege and by virtue of family or work, they take on signs and images that in the popular consciousness isolate them from the establishment. According to Baudrillard, this mode of "[d]ifferentiation may then take the form of the rejection of objects, the rejection of 'consumption,' and yet this still remains the very ultimate in consumption" (ibid.). Marta, challenged by her cynical friend Manuel to reevaluate her ideological commitment, wonders if her claim to Marxism is reflected in the fact that her wealthy parents had given her a Lada, a Russian car, as a present rather than some other car that is associated with the establishment: "¿en qué consistía pertenecer a ese sector? . . . ¿en que sus padres le hubieran regalado un Lada en lugar de un Honda Civic?" (what did belonging to that sector mean? that her parents had given her a Lada rather than a Honda Civic for a present?) (60).

As for Carlos, it is all in his manner or demeanor. He rides a

Vespa rather than own a car, and he goes around carrying an old, worn canvas bag. In his own opinion the Vespa and the old bag make him look like a mailman. Santiago, obviously "underconsuming," chooses to live in an apartment he describes as "un piso viejo, casi de estudiante, donde pagaba un alquiler bastante por debajo de sus posibilidades" (an old student-type apartment, where the rent was well below his means) (29). Ironically, by living below his means he is able to save up four million pesetas to lend to Carlos. This act, he admits, "significaba que él era un igual, que era, como Marta, alguien nacido de pie" (meant that he was an equal, that he was, like Marta, someone born with a silver spoon in his mouth) (ibid.). His comfortable financial situation notwithstanding, he prefers to dress up in his late father's flannel pants and Tergal shirt when he visits Murcia, his hometown, on holidays. These clothes, to which he casually refers as "un disfraz" (a disguise) (28), are the real signs of his humble beginnings, of the family-owned bar, of memories of the sudden death of his father and "la angustia económica" (financial distress) (ibid.). However, Santiago, by means of spatial and emotional distancing, and more importantly, by deliberately underconsuming through putting on those signs of his humble beginnings, is able to reduce the real to the level of mere representation. Hence, although "Seguían allí, Murcia seguía allí" (They were still there, Murcia was still there) (ibid.), that world might just as well be a postcard image, a folkloric image (stripped of all historical reference for the immediate consumption and gratification of the tourist) in which he can participate by simply dressing up. His solidarity with his origins, and by extension with the underprivileged in society, is achieved through the performance of his origins during his visits to his hometown and it is no more genuine than is his identity as a socialist. Like Marta driving a Lada and Carlos dressed like a mailman, he also performs his left-wing identity.

The three friends' self-definition through acts of consumption undermines the integrity of their identity, for by means of this system of identity formation, they buy into the very system from which they attempt to alienate themselves. More importantly, their identity thus produced is rather tenuous, and as such they lack the freedom and the necessary tension between them and society required to effect change. The impotence of the consuming subject is underlined by the following observation made by Guillermo, Marta's husband, on his social group:

> [T]ristes de nosotros, intelectuales por horas sometidos a una profesión, tipificados en secciones censales con un habitat, un estatus, un estilo de consumo, un perfil . . . "Son los que más leen diarios de información general, tanto en días laborales como en fines de semana. Escuchan algo de radio convencional y de fórmula." (248)

> [Poor us, paid intellectuals subjected to a profession, typified in the census sections with a habitat, a status, a style of consumption, a profile . . . "They are the ones who read the general information daily newspapers most both on weekdays and on weekends. They listen to a bit of conventional radio."]

Sadly, as consuming subjects, their very identity is defined and determined by marketing surveys and similarly, their needs and their lifestyles are influenced by the same marketing strategies that were used to categorize them in the first place.

Carlos eloquently sums up the unraveling of the myth of the autonomous self in their consumer-oriented environment by contrasting the verb "elegir" (to choose), the action of the truly free subject, with the verbal phrase "tomar decisiones" (to make decisions), the action taken by the subject who is acted upon by an external agent. As a result of his own experience of being taken over by the multinational company, Electra, Carlos resolves to give his son a future lesson on autonomy by explaining to him that "[t]omar decisiones era sólo escoger entre los deseos de un muestrario concebido por el apetito propio o ajeno, casi siempre ajeno" (making decisions means choosing what one wants from a collection of samples conceived of by oneself or by somebody else, almost always by somebody else) (221). He elaborates:

> Le contaría que en eso había consistido su vida: decidir sin elegir, componer discursos para imitar a la razón, fingiendo que cada individuo en solitario tenía la insólita capacidad de convertir en racional el acto de haber comprado aquella chaqueta, de haber enviado a su hijo a este colegio, de haber vendido una pequeña empresa . . . Si nos van bien las cosas, tu madre y yo decidiremos qué piso comprar para que tú lo heredes y dejaremos de pensar en quién vas a ser tú. Dejaremos de creer que eso puede elegirse un poco. . . . Entre tu madre y yo ganare-

mos dinero para llevarte a un colegio que te proporcione los contactos suficientes, me situaré bien. No lo he elegido pero estoy decidiéndolo, así es cómo funciona, hijo, y el resto, la historia, . . . el sentido de ser hombres y poder juzgar, el resto existe, Diego, es un espejo sin luz. (ibid.)

[I would tell him that that is what his life had been: deciding without choosing, making speeches to imitate reason, pretending that each individual, alone, had the unusual ability to rationalize the act of buying that jacket, of sending his son to this school, of buying a small company . . . If things go well for us, your mother and I will decide what apartment to buy for you to inherit and we will stop worrying about what you are going to become. We will stop believing a little bit that that sort of thing can be chosen . . . Between your mother and me, we will earn money to put you in a private school that will provide you with enough contacts. I will position myself well. I have not chosen it but I am deciding it; that is how it works, son, and the rest, history, . . . the sense of being men and being able to judge, the rest exists, Diego, it is a dark mirror.]

In the above quotation, Carlos draws attention to the diminished role of individual choice in the identification process and the ascendancy, on the other hand, of external factors such as social contacts and social class as determinants of the self. As such, what his son is going to be, his true self, has nothing to do with his choices from a scale of values. It has to do, rather, with the decisions made on where he lives, where he goes to school, which movies he watches, which clothes he wears and similar activities that are typical of the externally determined subject.

As their self-determined identities give way to their consumer identities, the perceived boundaries between themselves and the "hostile" environment is threatened while the links they claimed to have formed with others of like mind are eroded. Within the new economic order that is replicated in the loan, Gopegui's characters are suddenly shown to be ungrounded, confused, and powerless. Previous relations—social, economic, political—are thrown into disarray; former ideological positions acquired during their university education lose their currency or are contested in an environment that is engulfed in the ever-extending boundaries of global commodity production and consumption.

The loan changes the dynamics of the relationship among the

three and obliges them to confront critically the contradictions in their values. As a consequence their belief that they are above irrational, legitimizing, forces such as social class, family ties, and origin, becomes unraveled. The moment Marta and Santiago hand their checks to Carlos, their relationship is no longer governed by "amistad" (friendship). In spite of themselves they have become lenders and debtors to each other. The first source of identification that is revealed to be fragile within this new arrangement is the group. The loan reveals the contradictions in two assumptions surrounding group identitification. The first is the supposed autonomy of the members within the group with respect to the world outside of it. The second is the semblance of homogeneity among the members and the absence of fundamental social differences among them.

The semblance of homogeneity that bound the three friends in this novel together unravels when the significance of the loan to each of them individually is scrutinized. For Santiago, the four million pesetas were his entire life's savings. As a result he had more to lose in remaining true to the Marxist principles. Therefore, he muses "Disponer de un argumento para no prestarle los millones quizá le hubiese causado alivio" (Having an excuse to not lend him the millions might have given him some relief) (46). Indeed, Carlos's later request for an extension for repaying the loan threatened Santiago's beliefs even further, because by that time he had even more to lose. Having the extra four million pesetas in his account provided him with the means to meet his daily needs. More importantly for him, however, it also gave him the confidence to pursue a woman who was wealthier than he was but through whom he saw more doors opening for him (81). Therefore, although his response to the request was "Tranquilo, no te preocupes" (Don't worry) (82), his unspoken reaction was "¡Qué putada, Carlos, justo ahora, justo cuando necesitaba dinero por el amor!" (What a pain, Carlos! such bad timing; just when I needed money for love!) (ibid.). Marta, on the other hand, recognizes that "Santiago se había jugado algo con el préstamo . . . Ella en cambio, siempre se jugaba menos. Ella tenía unos padres dispuestos a socorrerla y con dinero para hacerlo si se daba el caso" (Santiago had taken quite a risk with that loan . . . She on the other hand, had risked far less. She had parents who were willing to come to her aid and who had the money to do so if it became necessary)

(50). Conscious of the imbalance of power and privileges among them as friends and within the movement as a whole, Marta doubts the legitimacy of her claim to belong to the group as she wonders "[c]ómo sería . . . vivir con el cuidado de que el día se cumpliera y no con las pasiones, los deseos, de quien ya lo tiene cumplido" (I wonder what it would be like . . . to live with the anxiety that one's daily needs are met and not with the passions, the desires, of someone who already has everything) (51).

The loan not only reveals the imbalance of power and privileges, as well as divergent motivations of the members of the group, but also the fallacy of the feeling of autonomy and separation from the hostile world outside, governed by irrational and arbitrary principles. Upon close scrutiny, it is evident that Marta, Santiago, and Carlos are in reality microcosms of the entities from which they claimed to be alienated. Their actions are governed by principles that are no less interested than those that rule the workings of the market, the banks, the state and the big businesses. No longer protected by the savings of four million pesetas in the bank, and threatened by a possible layoff as a result of impending elections, Marta accepts a job as "asesora [consultant] en la Dirección General de Coordinación Técnica Comunitaria," although she is opposed to the Maastricht Treaty (177). She admits to Manuel that in her new position, "no voy a admitir que intentaré aportar algo distinto desde dentro, porque no creo que se pueda" (I am not going to admit that I will try and contribute something different from within, because I don't think that is possible) (ibid.). She appears to be aware that by accepting that job, she had also accepted that there was a wedge between her personal sense of progress and the common good of the society.

Similarly, Carlos, who is in a vulnerable postion as a debtor and who is aware of the adverse impact of the loan on the personal lives of his friends and on his relationship with them, sells Jard off to Electra for exactly eight million pesetas, which go to Santiago and Marta:

[É]l había antepuesto la turbia aprobación de Santiago Álvarez y Marta Timoner a las necesidades de Rodrigo, de Esteban. Su deuda estaba antes, pero él podría haberla aplazado y seguir debiendo dinero a Santiago y a Marta durante años . . . [É]l se encontró tomando partido por Santiago y por Marta, pues el reproche de Rodrigo y Esteban no le dolería tanto como la perpetua condescendencia de sus amigos, de sus iguales. (285)

[He had given priority to the vague approval by Santiago Álvarez and Marta Timoner rather than to the needs of Rodrigo and Esteban. Yes, his debt came up first, but he could have postponed paying it and continued to owe Santiago and Marta for years . . . He found himself taking sides with Santiago and Marta because Rodrigo's and Esteban's disapproval would not hurt him as much as the perpetual indulgence of his friends, his equals.]

As we have seen, by giving the loan to Carlos, Santiago puts himself in a weak position in his relationship with Leticia, a wealthy woman. For further financial security he accepts to teach a masters course. It is only when he gets his money back from Carlos that he is able to turn down a position at a private university, ostensibly guided by his integrity:

No me gusta que me paguen como si diera conferencias cuando en realidad yo sería un profesor más . . . Tendrían que dejarme organizar el área de conocimiento, pero tampoco allí dentro hay gente interesante con quien trabajar. (273)

[I don't like them paying me as if I were an invited speaker when in reality I would be just another professor . . . They would have to allow me to organize the area of study, but there aren't interesting people with whom to work there either.]

When pressed further by Leticia, though, it becomes clear that money, and not the common social good, is the ultimate determinant in whether or not he follows through with his ideological obligations. When she challenges him by reminding him that "[p]ero diste un máster" (but you taught a masters course), his response is "[e]n ese momento necesitaba dinero" (at that time I needed money) (ibid.).

The contradictions implied in an identity based on the group reveal what the three friends experience as the disappearance of a credible and effectual left-wing organization. As Santiago laments, seemingly unaware of his own role in the state of affairs, "[l]a multitud se había dispersado" (the masses had dispersed) (46).We are informed that "Santiago había formado parte de aquella multi-

tud, y había tenido la impresión de que existía un relevo permanente: aun cuando tú dejaras de hacer algo, otro lo haría, igual que
tú harías lo que otro hubiera dejado de hacer" (Santiago had belonged to those masses, and he had had the impression that there
was a permanent process of replacement: even when you stopped
doing something, someone would do it in your place, in the same
way that you would if someone else were to give up) (45).

The dispersion of the group is clearly evident in what had become of another cohort of young activists that Guillermo, Marta's
husband, was hoping to join. This other set of friends "intentaba
crear su propia fundación: ganarse la vida fuera y, en la fundación,
hacer estudios orientados a la acción política" (tried to create their
own foundation: earn their living outside, while within the foundation they would pursue studies geared toward political action)
(247). However, they appear to have discovered the ubiquity of
the market principle, and they announce to him when he goes to
his first meeting: "Vamos a disolvernos" (We are going to break
up) (ibid.). What happens to this group mirrors what is happening
to the three friends and their acquaintances: "Una de las chicas
había conseguido una plaza de profesora en Asturias. Otra tenía
un contrato de colaboradora en una empresa donde, sin embargo,
trabajaba nueve o diez horas diarias . . . Quedaban dos chicos y
una chica más, pero iban a constituirse una empresa" (One of the
girls had got a position as a professor in Asturias. Another girl had
obtained a contract as a collaborator in a company; however, she
had to work nine or ten hours daily . . . There were two boys and
a girl left, but they were going to set up a company) (247–48).

The disintegration of the group challenges the fundamentals of
modern Western thinking, championed by the middle class and articulated previously by Santiago. According to these principles,
one is able to improve oneself and the world through one's own
effort as though one were insulated against intrusion from any external force. Santiago and his friends had tried to forge an identity
based on their own choices rather than on an imposed set of
choices. However, the contradictions in their identity founded on
that of the group reveal their lack of agency and suggest that they
are all victims of what the author calls in her prologue the "mecanismos que empañan la hipotética libertad del sujeto" (mechanisms that undermine the hypothetical freedom of the subject)
(12). They are confronted with the realization that their identities,

which hitherto had hinged on their integration into or marginalization from various autocratic institutions, have shifted imperceptively into areas where they are determined no longer by themselves and their relationship to others but rather by forces outside of the self. In an e-mail message to Marta, Santiago eloquently sums up the nature of this ontological conflict in terms of the existence or not of God and by calling into question his previously professed materialism:

> Si Dios no existe, si no hay una última instancia entonces somos responsables de nuestros actos . . . Si Dios no existe, Marta, tendríamos que poder explicar por qué hoy es viernes y todavía ni yo ni . . . tú hemos llamado a Carlos . . . Todo lo que detestamos, Marta, la crueldad gratuita, la incontinencia, la mezquindad, cualquier acto ruin podría ser redimido en aras de la interpretación si hay un ojo que todo lo ve. Y eso, Marta, fue Dios. (287)

> [If God does not exist, if there isn't an ultimate institution then we are responsible for our actions. If God does not exist, Marta, we would have to explain why today is Friday and still neither I nor you have phoned Carlos . . . Everything that we detest, Marta, gratuitous cruelty, self-gratification, pettiness, any despicable act could be forgiven for the sake of understanding if there is an eye that sees everything. And that, Marta, used to be God.]

In this seeming rejection of his professed atheism, Santiago wavers in his belief in the power of the self to make and interpret reality. He postulates that if there is no agent external to the self, then the subject is ultimately responsible for its actions and their consequences and for explaining all phenomena. To him, this is the meaning of the absence of God. It also means that if there is no agent beyond the self that determined actions and their consequences, one should be able to rationalize one's actions and give meaning to one's existence. This materialist way of thinking gives the subject control of itself and of its world. It is reflected in the bourgeois social vision that Santiago admits earlier that he shares: "voluntarismo pequeñoburgués o la creencia en el mérito propio, en el esfuerzo individual como instrumento para corregir las injusticias de la lucha de clases" (that petit bourgeois belief in willpower or self-worth, in the virtue of individual effort as a means of correcting the injustices in the class struggle (63). But this notion is undermined through Santiago's own realization that both he and Marta are unable to find rational reasons and explanations for their actions. One can extend Santiago's questions around the absence or the presence of God further to include other actions and desires that are inexplicable to characters in the novel: Why did Santiago and Marta agree to lend the money to Carlos? Why did Carlos borrow the money from them rather than go to the banks? Why did they want the money back? Why did Santiago leave his girlfriend Sol for a wealthier woman, Leticia? The answers lie in the nature of that external agent of determination.

Consequently, individual interests rather than social cohesion take over as the driving force of their actions. This is evident in the personal turmoil that assails both Marta and Santiago after they lend the money to Carlos. It is clear that personal acts of self-actualization—what one would call lifestyle—appear to be in conflict with social loyalties. Santiago is irritated with Carlos for borrowing his four million pesetas because in doing so Carlos had deprived him of his freedom to pursue a certain lifestyle. As he observes in the following statement, in which he reflects on the real impact on his existence of the money Carlos returns to him, his loyalty to Carlos comes second place to his personal freedom. He regrets that in the latter's moment of need, "Carlos había estado solo . . . Por unos cuantos brunches y un par de vacaciones exóticas, por compartir un motor 2,3 litros de 158 caballos de vapor . . . por eso había cometido aquella abyección trivial, no llamar a Carlos" (Carlos had been alone . . . For a few brunches and a couple of exotic vacations, for sharing a 2.3 litre motor with 158 horsepower . . . for that he had committed that trivial, wretched act, not calling Carlos) (284). For Marta, the loan she gave to Carlos resulted in a lot of anxiety and frustration when she realizes that it greatly compromised her lifestyle. Without immediate access to the four million pesetas, she and her husband, Guillermo, will not be able to afford their dream house, an old house in Madrid, where Guillermo will be able to indulge his hobby in renovations. She recognizes that she was willing to give to Carlos "[s]ólo aquella cantidad que no le supusiera ningún cambio significativo" (only the amount that would not impact significantly on her) (113). In both instances the frustration that the two friends feel is due to the fact that they see the loan to Carlos as jeopardizing their desire for self actualization; self-actualization that, interestingly, excludes the other of like mind.

The consuming habit of the characters may give them a semblance of freedom, but that individualized freedom is incompatible with other social relationships by which they had previously defined themselves, hence the sense of loneliness, despite apparent social associations, that permeates the characters' lives. The following observation made by Dunn regarding the subject in the consumer society serves as an explanation for the aloneness of the characters in *La conquista del aire* and also explains the characteristic tendency toward individualism in the novels of this generation in general:

> Consumer individualism, additionally, serves as a pale imitation of "authentic" individualism based on values of achievement and individual self-worth. Consumer choice, in this view, has replaced real social and political recognition, trivializing freedom through its reduction to the category of taste. Consumerism, to the extent that it privatizes choice by enforcing loyalty to the values of leisure and lifestyle, has a depoliticizing effect, turning workers—who might otherwise be solidaristic and militant—into consumers, and citizens—who might otherwise engage in collective action—into spectators. (1998, 69)

Marta sums up their aloneness when she muses on the disintegration of their friendship: "¿Por qué en vez de estar juntos, quizá también con Santiago, hablando de Carlos, de su empresa y de cómo podían ayudarle, por qué tenían que estar separados hablando cada uno del otro? Marta resistía y por fin decidió no llamar a nadie, quedarse en casa oyendo música y leyendo" (Why was it that, instead of being together, perhaps with Santiago too, talking about Carlos and his company and how they could help him, they had to be talking separately about one another? Marta resisted and finally decided not to call anyone and to remain at home listening to music and reading) (163). Clearly, as each of them strives—unable to escape the claws of the market—to define himself or herself according to consumer values, their allegiance to the common cause wanes. The price for their freedom to be themselves, that is, to indulge in the middle-class values of personal tastes, leisure, and lifestyle, is their aloneness, as Marta discovers when she sits in business class on her way to Cologne on a business trip: "Saldría del aeropuerto y nadie la aguardaría, y nadie sabría en parte alguna lo que estaba siendo de Marta. Qué transparente y fría era la libertad" (She would walk out of the airport and no one would be waiting for her, and no one anywhere would know what was becoming of Marta. Freedom was so transparent and cold.) (193). All the characters, thus, suffer from an aloneness which reflects the social and cultural impact of Spain's transformation into a modern consumer society as described by Graham and Sánchez: "Spain's transformation into a modern consumer society over the last thirty years has meant the erosion of traditional forms of social and political solidarity and the predominance of money in a hierarchy of social values . . . 'Monetarized' cultural values, inevitably translate human worth into pure exchange or production value" (1995, 414).

The current condition of the subject in the market economy as shown in the experiences of the characters in *La conquista del aire*, I believe, is what prompts Gopegui to wonder in the prologue of the novel if it is possible these days to write "una novela de aprendizaje" (a bildungsroman) (13), that is, a novel with a hero opposing unacceptable social or political practices in the course of his or her development. She explains that as money has become such an inextricable part of the subject in its socialization, and since the subject has internalized what she calls the "libro de órdenes de nuestro tiempo" (the regulations of our time) (13), the subject is not in the position to enter into conflict with opposing sets of values. Her protagonist in *Lo real* articulates further this sense of entrapment in the mercantile economy when he explains to his wife the futility of attempting to live on the margins of the corrupting tyranny of the market:

> Y vivir como si no hiciera falta corromperse . . . Como si uno pudiera ir al monte con unas cabras a vender quesos ecológicos. Ésa es la trampa. Creer que uno puede elegir, que el dinero con que compras las cabras no sale de ningún sitio. (290)

> To live as if it were not necessary to corrupt oneself . . . As if one could go up to the mountains with some goats and sell organic cheese. That was the trap. To think that one can choose, that the money one used to buy the goats came from nowhere.]

There seems to be no outlet then for the subject but nihilism. However, in her characteristic Marxist discourse, elsewhere in an article, "Ser infierno," which reads like the thesis of *Lo real* and *La conquista del aire* (indeed parts of the article are repeated in *Lo real*), Gopegui speaks of the need to have the courage to not accept what things say they are but rather look for what they really are—rather like looking beneath the surface of things for what is "real," as in the title of her novel *Lo real*. This is what she sets out to do in both novels; she scratches the surface of Spain's young democratic environment and sees that the only freedom that exists is what she cynically calls in the same article "la libertad de ser explotado, la única libertad que conocemos, la única que nos da señas de identidad" (the freedom to be exploited, the only freedom that we know, the only one that gives us identity) (2000b, 29). This is a rather harsh indictment of the nature of contemporary democracies controlled by pecuniary interests.

Belén Gopegui's response to the dilemma faced by the characters in *La conquista del aire* is the alternative hero in the person of the protagonist of *Lo real,* Edmundo Gómez. On the surface, Edmundo is hardly the character to be considered as the personification of the indictment against the system. He is an unapologetic liar, cheat, blackmailer, schemer, and plotter, as well as an opportunist who defines himself as "un ateo del bien" (a nonbeliever in goodness), but who, however, holds what is considered a respectable position in society. To condemn Edmundo's activities as immoral is to assume that the referent against which one measures his activities upholds the moral standards the rest of society is supposed to follow. However, the world in which Edmundo operates, that is the world of mass-media corporations and modern politics, the world supposed to epitomize the change from dictatorship to democracy, is no paragon of truth either. That world also thrives on an official version of reality designed to maintain power rather than to empower.

The deception hidden in what is held to be absolute truth is revealed in Edmundo's own role in the government referendum on Spain's relationship to NATO. On the surface the government encouraged public participation in national decision making by calling a referendum to determine whether Spain should remain in NATO or withdraw from the organization. Behind the scenes, however, marketing consultants charged with controlling the relationship between the public and consumer goods are contracted by the government to assist it to obtain a yes vote in the referendum. It is noteworthy that Edmundo had previously worked for the same consulting firm. The consultants were hired to study "las características de ambos grupos con la vista puesta en la posibilidad de obtener una mayoría favorable a la permanencia en la OTAN" (the characteristics of both groups with a view to obtaining a majority that supports Spain remaining in NATO) (262). On the basis of their report on the profile of voters, the "Yes" campaign in favor of Spain's continued membership in NATO is taken on by a communications agency which supervised the designing of slogans, television adverstisements, and the organization of meetings to secure the results desired by the PSOE.

The perversion of democracy by the government's use of marketing strategies cannot be more evident. The ability to make a political choice based on one's independent convictions in this environment then, is no less farcical than the idea that the consumer has unlimited choices. Edmundo points out that, as a market analyst, it is his job to study consumers' attitudes in order to arrive at the best way to influence their choices. His aim in studying market surveys is not to ultimately provide the public with its choices or with its particular needs but rather to influence the choices it makes: "procuraría no creerme las encuestas . . . Dedicaría ese tiempo a preguntarme si se puede cambiar algo para hacer que a alguien le importe bastante lo que sólo le importa un poco" (I would try not to believe in surveys . . . I would spend that time wondering if anything could be changed to make someone care a lot about something that he or she only cares a little about) (196–97). It is suggested in this novel that the freedom to choose, one of the so-called truths of 1990s Spain, whether the cereal one wants to eat or the nature of one's government, is but a sham, and so are many other such truths that are called into question by Edmundo.

The task confronting Gopegui's alternative hero in *Lo real* then, is not to put himself in the position of one who denounces corrupt political or social practices, for this will imply attempting to pitch what is considered to be universal truths against similar universal truths. In this context, in which even democracy is perverted, similar truths (not necessarily related to commonly repudiated and outmoded practices such as political dictatorships) are questionable. Therefore, Edmundo's freedom, or rather his heroic act, is best achieved through his role as a divulger of what is hidden rather than as a combatant on behalf of what is supposedly the truth or absolute reality. That is, his role is to unmask the fictitiousness of the official narrative to reveal the nature of the freedom of the subject in the so-called democratic environment.

It is therefore not mere coincidence that Edmundo Gómez, who calls himself "un ateo del bien" (a non-believer in goodness) on one occasion, introduces himself as "Mefisto Gómez" (213) and carries around a copy of Joost van den Vondel's (1587–1679) play *Lucifer*. In his image as the "fallen angel," he incarnates the other half of all reality, which, to continue in the imagery of the Judeo-Christian tradition, was banished to the netherworld with Lucifer and the rest of the rebellious angels. Edmundo's objective then, is different from that of other "heroes" before him or even that of the characters of *La conquista del aire*. His objective is not to battle the forces of evil, whether totalitarian regimes or dehumanizing multinational companies, for in the new economic order, the values of the two are not separate. Neither is more truthful than the other. To wage battle against what he perceives to be "evil" within the limited reality will be nothing more than to operate within the parameters preestablished by the normative order. Furthermore, in the context of a limited reality, the normative meaning of all values is questionable. Goodness, loyalty, friendship, truth, honesty, humility, modesty, and hard work—these values, whose meanings are located in the sites of power, are tenable only in the context of a limited or mutilated reality.

Edmundo, aka Mefisto, organizes the spaces that he inhabits to reflect his existence in incomplete realities. He acquires two living quarters: his official apartment on Balthazar Gracián Street and a clandestine one on Luca de Tena. In the former, there is no reference at all to his past shame and pain arising from his being the son of the disgraced and imprisoned MATESA employee who was involved in the famous scandal. That apartment only reflects his identity as a modern, successful professional; one who has succeeded, as the normative value system would have us believe, solely by dint of his hard work and his personality. The secret seventh-floor apartment on Plaza Luca de Tena, however, complements the first. It contains elements of the unspoken aspects of the official version of reality. In this apartment Edmundo keeps his archives of classified information on certain important personalities. The information may be seen simply as arsenal for blackmail;

indeed, he uses it for that purpose, as he said "para obtener a cambio un poco de la libertad que nadie le ofrecía" (to obtain in exchange a small amount of freedom that no one was offering him) (209). However, apart from its utilitarian value this information serves to complete the reality in which Edmundo has to live and work and, therefore, it gives him some power. The new economic order, like the old political regime, thrives on partial or manufactured reality, which is created through image manipulation or information management. Edmundo's operations in the apartment on Luca de Tena show an attempt to reveal total reality and in so doing appropriate the power wielded by the people or the institutions who control the official versions of "truths."

Beyond combining partial realities to obtain a more complete state of affairs, Edmundo's most innovative strike against false official narratives of democracy and freedom is achieved through his construction of his own version of untruths. He does this by means of reinventing himself and, contrary to expectations, thriving in his new fabricated self. In doing so, he turns the normative meaning of what is good and what is considered bad on its head. Indeed on the level of objective vital experiences, Edmundo had faced rejection in various relationships—personal and professional—and therefore arrives at the conclusion, according to Irene Arce, the narrator, that "No le necesitaban" (He was not needed) (153). In reaction to this realization, he decides to "diseñar a un tipo como el que necesitaban" (design a guy who was like the person they needed) (153). As Edmundo Gómez, son of disgraced and imprisoned government employee, he felt that he had been rejected by friends and peers and two girlfriends. Similarly, as Edmundo Gómez, middle-level employee in a medical laboratory that was given more to profit generation and competition than to employee or consumer satisfaction, he was not highly valued by his employers. He even felt rejected by his own mother, who in his opinion would have preferred a son capable of making up for the humiliation and failure suffered by his family (153). What each and every one of these people wanted was an illusion in that it existed only in theory or in the model created by middle-class values. They were trying to make him fit the image of the young, hardworking, middle-class male, who is not tarnished in any way by acts such as lying or stealing, which, on the surface, are considered reprehensible in the society.

Edmundo, as invented by Edmundo, is a simulacrum par excellence according to Baudrillard's interpretation of the term (1988, 167–68). He is not merely a reflection, a representation, a copy, or a mirror image of a real entity but rather a reproduction of the imaginary. Furthermore, like Baudrillard's notion of the simulacrum, he does not simply "feign" to be what he is not. That, according to Baudrillard, would amount to simply placing a mask over what is real. In this instance, however, he does not merely wear a mask; rather he actually reproduces in himself the signs of the imaginary entity that he wishes to be. To become that successful, aggressive, postindustrial communications and marketing executive, he goes so far as to simulate the Western-style education of such an individual. He does not only lie about going to study for a master's degree in the United States but also designs for himself a curriculum "idóneo para los nuevos altos cargos de las empresas de comunicación" (that was ideal for the new high positions in the media corporations) (154). In his invented study plan he hoped to learn the techniques of creating and budgeting for television programs, study both conservative and progressive theories in the field, and acquire some knowledge in the humanities which he had heard was currently common in the business programs. Furthermore, in keeping with course requirements in the field, he planned to invent and actually write papers that would have been expected of him. He even goes so far as to plan to invent the profile of his teachers and peers, and with a false CV he does an internship with a radio station in Belfast (171).

The outcome of this process of simulation and deception is the individual who is able to hold his own and successfully hold a number of executive positions first in a market research company and then in Televisión Española. Edmundo's success is no doubt a direct result of his ability to function in the context and on the level of representations of democracy. In this context, the subject appears to exercise the democratic right to choose, as demonstrated through public opinion polls, but in reality, it is beholden to the dictates of money. Edmundo is Gopegui's response to the threat posed by economic totalitarianism to the individual's autonomy and freedom. Edmundo opts to become, as has been mentioned earlier, an "ateo del bien," thus exercising his privilege to at least choose an alternative to the sanctioned ethics on conduct.

In both *La conquista del aire* and *Lo real* Belén Gopegui focuses on characters whose agency, contrary to expectation, is either undermined or threatened in the market-driven environment of 1990s Spain. The recurrent theme of the characters' inability to choose their destiny openly contradicts expectations in light of Spain's image at the time as a democratic and even affluent European country. The characters of the first novel find themselves ill equipped to challenge the "market dictatorship." Indeed, they discover that they have been absorbed and molded by that environment. The central character of *Lo real,* on the other hand, is in a sense a foil to those of the previous novel. Through his own machinations to manipulate reality, he reveals the conflation of media, market, and government to further demonstrate the perversion of freedom. Through these characters, Gopegui suggests that the freedom they supposedly enjoy in the democratic environment is vacuous. The reality is that the source of their domination has merely shifted from the political sphere to that of economics. This is the particular reality of 1990s Spain as perceived by Belén Gopegui in spite of the celebrations of progress and affluence promoted by the government of the time.

4

Inventing the Author: Antonio Orejudo Utrilla in *Fabulosas narraciones por historias* and *Ventajas de viajar en tren*

THE NOVELS THAT HAVE BEEN EXAMINED SO FAR DEMONSTRATE THEIR authors' concern with the undermining of the individual's authority in the cultural and socioeconomic context of 1990s Spain in various ways, which include the following: an engagement with media and commodity transformations of identity (*Historias del Kronen* and *La pistola de mi hermano*), illustrations of diminished agency in the postcapitalist or informational society (*De Madrid al cielo* and *Veo veo*), and the criticism of the market's absorption of an ineffectual 1990s middle class (*La conquista del aire* and *Lo real*). Antonio Orejudo Utrilla articulates this recurrent preoccupation from a generational perspective. He does so through two metafictional novels that focus on the impact of the media-dominated, market-controlled context on the authority of the author himself or herself.

Orejudo Utrilla captures in *Fabulosas narraciones por historias* and *Ventajas de viajar en tren* the ambiguities, contradictions, and paradoxes that contribute to destabilizing the concept of the author as authority with regard to this incipient generation. Like his compatriot don Miguel de Cervantes four centuries before him, Antonio Orejudo Utrilla treads the fine line between creation and criticism in fiction by turning these two novels to gaze upon themselves and upon the fiction of his time. In so doing, he offers an ironic view of the literary environment within which his own generation of novelists practiced their craft. Orejudo Utrilla weighs in on the ongoing concern with the contemporary concept of author and the related issue of the value of contemporary Spanish fiction by examining in both *Fabulosas narraciones por historias* and

Ventajas de viajar en tren the process of canonization of the author and the value of first-person narration when the "authority" of author is questionable. Orejudo Utrilla suggests in these two novels that the notion of author of a novel is itself an element of fiction created by external forces such as market demands. This idea, he suggests, is not incompatible with the literary value of a work. It only becomes so when there is an attempt to deny the fictionality of the concept of author by ignoring the external factors that mediate between his or her image and the work in question.

An initial examination of Orejudo Utrilla's parody of the aethetization of youth among the Generation of 1927 and in the cultural environment of the 1920s in *Fabulosas narraciones por historias* will throw light on the fundamental theme of these two metafictional novels: that literature production and consumption today, and by extension the creators of literature, are not entirely independent of the market and other extraliterary forces. I will then show that, with this in mind, Orejudo Utrilla discredits the canonization of authors that traditionally has served to suggest an author's authority or autonomy. Furthermore, having suggested that the concept of author is as fictional as the work of fiction itself, Orejudo Utrilla exposes the contradiction in his generation's insistence on the first-person narrative. This subjective narrative form suggests an "authorization" that Generation X novelists cannot claim to possess if they are consciously exposing their manipulation by external forces. As an alternative to the first-person authoritarian voice, Orejudo Utrilla offers multiple unreliable narrative voices.

The events that make up *Fabulosas narraciones por historias* are set primarily in the early twentieth century between 1923 and the end of the Spanish civil war. This observation is based on a reference in the novel to Primo de Rivera's coup d'etat (*Fabulosas narraciones* 20; future references will be given parenthetically by page number in the text) and on the fact that toward the end of the novel one of the principal characters, Santos, is said to be prospering in the Franco regime. However, the novel as a whole is closely linked to the 1990s through the letters that an initially unidentified person exchanges with the narrator. The first of these is signed in Belle Terre in July 1986 (19). The last, signed in the same city, is dated March 6, 1994 (515). Furthermore, in this last letter, the sender, who turns out to be a certain María Luisa de Babenberg, accuses the narrator of linguistic anachronism, which places his work in the 1990s rather than in the 1920s: "¿es que no se ha dado cuenta de que sus personajes hablan como los jóvenes de hoy y que tienen costumbres contemporáneas?" (haven't you realized that your characters speak like the young people of today and that they have contemporary habits?) (513). Ironically, the letters that she herself supposedly wrote to the narrator about the cultural environment of the twenties are also full of references that are suspiciously applicable to the context of 1990s Spain. Among these references are the frequent allusions to the aesthetization of youth in the culture of the twenties. In one of her descriptions of the twenties she writes that "[l]a economía iba muy bien, y eso se traducía en entusiasmo, jamones, alegría y juventud, mucha juventud. La juventud era un valor en alza en aquellos años" (the economy was doing very well and that was reflected in enthusiasm, ham, joy and youth, a lot of youth. The value of youth was on the rise in those years) (17). In another letter she elaborates further:

> Sí es cierto que había pocos jóvenes y que los cuatro que había tenían desde edad temprana ansias de edad provecta; pero creo que es precisamente esa escasez la que explica el rango metafísico que la juventud alcanzó entre nosotros. La juventud y todo lo que ella trae consigo de inexperiencia, frescura, ingenuidad y violencia se alzaron a la categoría de valores estéticos. (167)

> [Yes, it's true that there were few young people and those few, from very early on, yearned for maturity; but I think that it is precisely that scarcity that explains the metaphysical level that youth attained among us. Youth and all that it brings with it, such as inexperience, cheek, innocence and violence, were raised to the level of aesthetic values.]

This observation is reiterated in the criticism by Tuñidor, one of the many literary critics who appear in the novel, of the supposed value placed on youth in the literary circles of the 1920s:

> Estoy hasta el gorro de esta glorificación exagerada y absurda de la juventud que padecemos. Hoy día no importa la calidad de la obra de arte. Lo único que interesa es la edad de su autor y lo irreverente que pueda ser para con sus mayores. Estoy en total desacuerdo con esta política. (121)

[I have had it with this exaggerated and absurd glorification of youth we have to put up with. Today the quality of the work of art does not matter. The only thing of interest is the author's age and how irreverent he can be with his elders. I totally disagree with this policy.]

The above-mentioned characters appear to be referring to the Generation of 1927 poets. The representative poets of the Generation of 1927 not only earned critical acclaim as young innovative writers but also paid homage to and celebrated youth and what it stood for in their poetry. They contributed to the poetization of youth in all its manifestations in order to capture the cultural ambience of the Roaring Twenties and demonstrate their own quest for change and renewal in poetic expression. Although youth is one of the distinguishing characteristics of the Generation of 1927, and although in Orejudo Utrilla's novel it is this generation of writers that is favored by the literary establishment, Tuñidor's and Luisa de Babenberg's comments could well have been elicited by the literary environment of 1990s Spain. Tuñidor's words, especially, resonate with the objections that some critics have raised in relation to the nineties when many young Spanish writers published their first novels.

By parodying the creation of the Generation of 1927 and their cultural environment, Orejudo Utrilla brings attention to bear on the so-called mercantile environment of the nineties and its role in the creation of a new generation of "young" writers. In Orejudo Utrilla's fictionalization, this revered generation had to rely on the manipulative and mercenary activities of some interested individuals, like Baron Leo Babenberg, to attain its status of a literary generation: "Se ve a la legua que Babenberg es un mecenas; pero en realidad es un comerciante que ha encargado a Ortega la creación de una generación literaria rentable a medio plazo, que dé dinero, lo único que le interesa" (You can tell from a mile away that Babenberg is a patron; but in reality he is a businessman who has entrusted Ortega with the creation of a literary generation that is profitable in the short term; that is the only thing that interests him) (232).

It appears that the fictional patron of the Generation of 1927 was forced by the consumers of literature of his time to resort to the commercial approach. This fictionalized Generation of 1927 had to compete, rather unsuccessfully, with the popular writers whose works were being devoured by the reading public. In her first letter to the narrator, in which she describes the literary climate of the 1920s, María Luisa de Babenberg, points out how ironic it is that the Generation of 1927 should enjoy canonical status today, for they were not read in their time:

> ¡Ah, Pepe Ortega! Tenemos que hablar de él. Pese a lo que digan los libros, no crea usted que en aquellos años todo el mundo leía a Pepe, a Juan Ramón, o que todos adoraban a Lorca; o que Unamuno era conocido por todos los españoles. Entonces la gente era como ahora. ¿Conoce hoy todo el mundo a García Hortelano, a Claudio Rodríguez, a Cela, a Juan Marsé o a ese chico joven, Eduardo Mendoza? No. Pues entonces, lo mismo. La gente leía a Álvaro Retana o a Alberto Insúa, autores de novelas que el público, la masa, como decía Pepe, devoraba. Paquito Ayala las llama ahora—lo he leído en sus memorias—novelas pornográficas. Supongo que se refiere al hecho de que podían vender hasta 100,000 ejemplares en una semana. A mí me encantaban. (19)

> [Ah, Pepe Ortega! We have to talk about him. In spite of what the books say, don't you believe that in those years everyone read Pepe, Juan Ramón, or that everyone adored Lorca; or that Unamuno was known by all Spaniards. At that time people were like they are today. Does everyone today know about García Hortelano, Claudio Rodríguez, Cela, Juan Marsé or that young man Eduardo Mendoza? No. Well, it was the same at that time. People read Álvaro Retana or Alberto Insúa, authors of novels that the public, the masses, as Pepe used to say, devoured. Paquito Ayala calls them—I read it in his memoirs—pornographic novels. I suppose he is referring to the fact that they could even sell 100,000 copies in a week. I loved them.][1]

It is being suggested here that despite the intervention of Babenberg and others, readers were drawn to the truly commercial writers. The challenge posed by the market, then, is not new. Then, as it is today, the so-called literary writers had to compete with the popular writers for readership.

Indeed, comments published by Generation X novelist Benjamín Prado concurs with the above suggestion that the presence of the market as a source of challenge to new writers is a generalized phenomenon. Prado suggests putting the accusations of the general corruption of the cultural climate in perspective. He concedes that "por supuesto que aquí y ahora hay una jauría de mentirosos y de oportunistas, cuando no de desalmados: hay autores de tercera jaleados por medios de comunicación afines, especialistas en pescar lo que no se merecen en el río revuelto de la prensa española" (of course, right now, there are a pack of liars and opportunists and even cruel people: there are third-rate writers urged on by similar communication media, specialists in claiming what they do not deserve in the messy world of the Spanish press).[2] However, he notes that "la existencia de escritores de poco mérito y mucha fama no es de hoy" (the existence of mediocre but famous writers is not new).[3] Like the fictional María Luisa de Babenberg, he goes on to cite concrete examples to show that writers of the caliber of Becquer and Juan Ramón Jimenez, who are held in high esteem today, would not have made the best-seller list if there was such a list in their time. Further examples like Rosa Chacel and Francisco Ayala, also today "unánimamente respetados" (unanimously respected), were not as widely read, he explains, "porque lo que arrasaba por aquella época en el mercado eran las novelas de *El Caballero Audaz* o las de Alberto Insúa, devorados hoy por las arenas movedizas del Tiempo" (what sold massively at that time were the novels of *El Caballero Audaz* or those of Alberto Insúa, which today have been devoured by the shifting sands of Time).[4] These examples are provided by Prado to support his point that the presence of, and the public taste for, popular and market-oriented culture over so-called high culture is not a new phenomenon in Spanish literature. More importantly, the seeming profusion of fiction promoted by the media and consumed by popular taste does not obliterate the presence of other kinds of literature that will endure the passage of time.

The Generation X novelists, however, perhaps caught in the neoliberal environment of 1990s Spain, write very self-consciously about their location in and manipulation by the market. In so doing they reveal the mechanisms that control their activities and expose their lack of autonomy as writers. By recreating a fictional version of the literary environment of the twenties in *Fabulosas narraciones por historias,* Orejudo Utrilla allows his readers to go behind the scenes of the production and distribution of culture in the contemporary environment. The result is the revelation of the ambiguity and the insecurity surrounding the existence of the author and his/her work in an environment destabilized by market interests. As seen in the activities of the fictionalized Generation of 1927 and in those of the less favored writers attempting to make a place for themselves, the literary field is located in an environment dominated by powerful forces that undermine the authority of authors.

Having revealed the hand of market interests in the creation of acceptable literature, Orejudo Utrilla suggests that the so-called established or canonized author is no more than "literatura" or pure representation. He does so in two ways in *Fabulosas narraciones por historias.* First, he reveals the transformation of real-life authors into artistic representations in the public consciousness. Second, he engages in the ironic reversal of such transformations from the public image to the real flesh-and-blood personality. In addition, he reiterates the notion of the invented author by drawing attention in both *Fabulosas narraciones por historias* and *Ventajas de viajar en tren* to the transformation of author into celebrity, one of the material means by which authority is invented.

In one of her letters to the anonymous novelist in *Fabulosas narraciones por historias,* María Luisa de Babenberg writes that in her experience, while "todos los esfuerzos de las criaturas de ficción van encaminados a convertirse en seres de carne y hueso" (all the efforts of the creatures of fiction are directed toward becoming beings of flesh and blood) (499), "los escritores, en cambio, seres de carne y hueso, hacen todo lo posible para convertirse en criaturas de ficción algún día: en estatuas, en billetes de banco, en sellos o en temas de libros escolares" (writers, on the other hand, who are beings of flesh and blood, are doing everything possible to turn into creatures of fiction one day: into bank bills, stamps or subjects of school books) (500). With these observations she anticipates Orejudo Utrilla's words in his "Nota del autor al lector" (A note from the author to the reader) (517), a kind of disclaimer at the end of the novel, to explain why his characters, although imaginary, have names of known literary and historical figures: "En nuestra imaginación de lectores aquellos hombres no son personas de carne y hueso, sino metáforas, ideas que habitan en el mismo mundo que don Quijote, Madame Bovary, Cervantes o Flaubert; criaturas de ficción que, en cierto modo, nos pertenecen a todos" (In our imagination as readers, those men are not people of flesh and blood but rather metaphors, ideas that inhabit the same world as Don Quixote, Madame Bovary, Cervantes or Flaubert; creatures of fiction who, in a certain way, belong to all of us) (517).

It is noteworthy that the two authors listed in this quotation have been grouped with the characters as fictional beings. These observations are accurate descriptions of the phenomenon of the writer's transformation in the public consciousness. Orejudo Utrilla captures in the inanimate medium of the bust of a writer gracing a park, or in his or her image etched in the popular consciousness through common media of exchange such as stamps or currency, the schism between the person and the artistic representation. Like the works of fiction that they are, these representations of the publicly accepted author, not unlike the hero of a novel, select and highlight aspects of the person that are deemed to be important by whoever creates the representation. They capture the greatness, the eminence, and the superiority of this represented figure above all others who do not find themselves thus immortalized. Furthermore, the very medium through which they are represented, as in the examples given by María Luisa de Babenberg, serve to add to their credibility as eminent contributors to the creation of Spanish culture. It would be unthinkable to challenge Galdós's image as the father of Spanish realism carved in the stone statue of a gently sleeping senior citizen, which adorns Retiro Park. No living author can measure up to Cervantes's immortalized image in several patrician statues that can be found all over Madrid.

Orejudo Utrilla thus encourages his reader to consider that figures of literary personalities used as role models and standards in judging the value of contemporary literature are not exactly "real." They are more often than not "fictional" portrayals. These fictional representations of authors are devoid of all references to human shortcomings and failings. They are sometimes detached from human and historical contexts and are often seen in the narrow framework of their success and significance to culture.

Orejudo Utrilla reveals the fictionalizing nature of authorization by reversing the process of transforming the flesh-and-blood individual into the canonized author as received by the reader. In *Fabulosas narraciones por historias*, a character named after Juan Ramón Jiménez, Nobel Prize winner (1956) and key figure in Spanish poetry in particular and in literature in general, bears the brunt of most of Orejudo Utrilla's iconoclastic revision of literary history. The standard bearer of "la poesía pura" (pure poetry), who sought to fuse imagery, words, and the very essence of beauty in his poetry, expresses himself in the most exaggerated Andalusian accent in Orejudo Utrilla's novel. Orejudo Utrilla's destruction of the received image of Juan Ramón Jiménez is most evident in the following passage, where ironically the latter criticizes fiction, realist fiction in particular, for being a portrayal of the reprehensible aspects of the human condition:

> La novela, hoy por hoy, ssarvo que vuerva ssu cabessa hassia lo inefable y sse haja lírica hatta en ssu lujareh má recónditoh, ettá llamá a dessaparessé, sse lo dijo sho, que ssoy conssehero de loh editoreh y de la revittah máh importanteh. Hoy por hoy, una novela realitta a lo don Benito Jarbanssero é impenssable. ¿Quién lee hoy por hoy ar pobre don Pío? Cuatro viehoh . . . No, essa novela humana, de arrabá, que paresse eccrita por mamíferoh y pa mamíferoh, indessente, má atenta a lo misserable que a lo intanhible, . . . hoy por hoy no tiene salía comerssial. (93)

> [Novels, today, except if you turn towards the ineffable and find lyricism in the most hidden place, is about to disappear, and I'm telling you this, as advisor to the most important publishers and magazines. Today, a realist novel in the style of Don Benito Chickpeas is unthinkable. Who reads poor Don Pío today? A bunch of old guys . . . No, that human novel, which seems to be written by mammals for mammals, indecent and more attentive to misery than to the intangible . . . today has no commercial value.]

The man of flesh and blood revealed in these words is a contradiction of the image of the poet captured in the fictionalizing medium of this advertisement posted at the Residencia de Estudiantes:

> El viernes, quince de septiembre, a las nueve de la noche, tendrá lugar una cena de homenaje y bienvenida al exquisito poeta y refinado prosista Juan Ramón Jiménez, . . . Asistirán a la suso mencionada cena: el ilustrísimo señor catedrático don Miguel de Unamuno, la más fuerte personalidad de la generación del 98; don José Ortega y Gasset, el incansable luchador por la europeización cultural de España. (25)

> [On Friday, the 15th of September, at 9 P.M., there will be a ceremonial dinner in honour of the exquisite and refined poet and prose writer, Juan Ramón Jiménez. . . . The following persons will be attending the above-mentioned event: the illustrious professor Don Miguel de Una-

muno, the strongest personality of the Generation of 98; Don José Ortega y Gasset, the tireless fighter for the Europeanization of Spanish culture.]

Versions of this advertisement of cultural events at the Residencia de Estudiantes appear three other times in the novel. Following the dinner in honor of Juan Ramón Jiménez, there was a talk to be delivered by Ortega y Gasset (113) and a class on the theme "Madre española e inmortalidad del Yo" (The Spanish mother and the immortality of the Ego) to be given by Unamuno (171). In addition, at Christmas there was going to be a Nativity recital presided over by the king and queen, accompanied by the "presidente de la junta" General Primo de Rivera (237). All the announcements of these events have a similar structure: the announcement of the event, followed by the introduction of the guest of honor described in lofty terms, followed by a list of other illustrious personalities from the world of Spanish history and culture, also described in superlative terms. Each announcement is very much the same as the previous one except for the introduction of a new guest of honor. In the last one, however, apart from the new guest of honor, there is a much longer list of cultural dignitaries: the older members of the Generation of 1927, Jorge Guillén and Pedro Salinas, as well as the younger members like Rafael Alberti, José Bergamín, and Vicente Aleixandre (238). Thus presented through repetitions of the same or similar epithets, the literary and cultural figures appear to the reader as immutable monuments or a series of static images, like portraits, in the pantheon of Spanish literature and culture. Noticeably, none of these "monuments" of Spanish culture include the image or a reference to female literary or cultural figures. Orejudo Utrilla's advertisements reflect the general predominance of males among those considered to be representative figures of literature and culture. They show the male/ masculine face of Spanish normative literary culture. This is further proof that literary history, like any other history, as a medium of representation and therefore a creation of the established writer, does not necessarily coincide with reality.

A further irony in the reproduction of the fossilized male-centered Spanish literary history is that all the writers who are presented here in Orejudo Utrilla's novel as monoliths, represented deviations from the norm in their time. They were voices of change, renewal, renovation, and innovation. In their canonized state, however, they have been transformed into bulwarks resisting change, and they do not reflect the plurality of reality. In other words, those who made their name as new voices go on to become the fictional personalities and the voices of Spanish literature and, therefore, they paradoxically resist change. This is what Patricio Cordero, one of the central characters in *Fabulosas narraciones por historias*, finds out when he tries in vain to publish his first novel, *Los Beatles*. He is rejected by the likes of Ortega y Gasset and Juan Ramón Jiménez because his novel deviated from the norms they have put in place.

To underline further the fictionalizing elements of the image of the established author, Orejudo Utrilla demystifies the process of authorization. He highlights the material means by which certain works and their writers attain the position of prominence and literary value by revealing the parallels between the celebrity formation process associated with popular culture and the process by which some highly regarded authors have come to be considered canons of Spanish literature. W in *Ventajas de viajar en tren*, for example, was a writer who was celebrated by the Left. Like the modern novelists, he has a personal relationship with his readership. The latter, as is often the case today, requires him, the tangible personality, the real-life person/author in order to complete the meaning of his works. Therefore, W, it appears, models his lifestyle on the expectations of his readership. For example, he thought that "para alguien muy leído por la izquierda resultaban muy apropiadas algunas prácticas eróticas que no estuvieran digamos muy extendidas entre la masa" (for someone who was read so much by the Left, it was very appropriate for him to have certain erotic habits that were not, let's say, common among the masses) (*Ventajas de viajar* 2000, 67; future references will be given parenthetically by page number in the text). That is, it was necessary for him to have certain eccentricities that will enable him to stand out and be recognized by his readers.

It is this need to transform the author into a known personality that, according to the narrator in *Ventajas de viajar en tren*, explains why, twenty years later, Helga Pato braves the elements to meet Martín Urales Úbeda, the impostor who had left her a red folder of narratives supposedly written by his patients at the mental institute:

[E]staba allí por curiosidad o por necesidad, por las mismas razones en todo caso que hacía veinte años la habían empujado a conocer en persona a W en la Feria del Libro en Frankfurt. Tal vez las mismas por las que había dedicado tantas energías a refutar para su inacabada tesis doctoral la autoría colectiva de la épica medieval, poniendo otra vez en circulación la vieja idea de un autor individual para cada obra. Soportaba el viento, la lluvia y el frío por la necesidad fetichista y enfermiza de que hubiese un ser humano detrás de las palabras. (141–42)

[She was there out of curiosity or need, in any case for the same reasons that had led her to go and meet W in person at the book fair in Frankfurt twenty years ago. Perhaps the same reasons that had led her to devote her energy toward refuting the idea of the collective authorship of the medieval epic in her unfinished doctoral thesis, putting into circulation again the old idea of an individual author for each work. She braved wind, rain and cold out of the fetishistic and sick need to find a human being behind the words.]

This need for an author to validate the work results in the conversion of the former into a personality, a celebrity like W, who in addition to writing "asistía a congresos, daba conferencias, hacía presentaciones y se acostaba ocasionalmente con alguna lectora" (attended conferences and gave lectures and presentations and occasionally slept with some female reader) (67).

One of the outcomes of the conversion of authors into celebrities according to Orejudo Utrilla is the tendency to confuse author with character. He comments on the confusion of author with character through Helga Pato in *Ventajas de viajar en tren*. The narrator tells the reader that "El problema de Helga Pato con las personas era que confundía a los narradores con los autores y a éstos algunas veces con los personajes" (Helga Pato's problem with people was that she confused narrators with authors and these with characters) (65). The narrator is quick to point out that Helga Pato is not a naive or uninformed reader. After all, she was "una veterana estudiante de doctorado a punto de terminar una polémica refutación de la autoría colectiva en la épica medieval" (a veteran PhD student who was about to conclude a controversial rebuttal of the notion of collective authorship in the medieval epic) (ibid.) when she met W in person at a book fair. To the narrator of *Ventajas de viajar en tren* the distinction between author and character should have been easy to make, especially for a person of Helga Pato's caliber. However, her thesis gives her away as a poor reader. She has transferred onto her reading of literature written during the Middle Ages, when the concept of author was indeed tenuous, a characteristic that is true of modern or post-modern literature. Helga Pato belongs to a generation for whom author, as material entity and creation, is necessary to validate the work. Hence it is not surprising that she took the step to meet W in Frankfurt. She approached him for an autograph, but he seduced her and she soon became his wife. No sooner had she met him than she wrote herself into his fiction: "Ella creyó que en ese momento comenzaba una novela de amor que trataba de una chica que decidía anular una beca de postgrado y abandonar la refutación de la autoría colectiva de la épica medieval" (She thought at that time that she was beginning a love story about a girl who decided to cancel a graduate scholarship and give up her rebuttal of the idea of collective authorship of the medieval epic) (65–66). Evidently Helga Pato had fallen into the trap of confusing writer with character: "Ella creyó que se casaba con su autor favorito, pero en realidad se había enamorado del narrador, y se casó con un personaje" (She thought that she was marrying her favorite author, but in reality she had fallen in love with the narrator, and she married a character) (66).

An examination of hints of contemporary literary practices leads one to fault Helga Pato less for confusing author, narrator, and character. For in both *Ventajas de viajar en tren* and *Fabulosas narraciones por historias*, Orejudo Utrilla undermines the secure image of the author as a "real" entity in an unreal world and underlines his or her fictionality. This is in keeping with the conviction that, according to him, led him to write *Ventajas de viajar en tren:* "La he escrito cansado de esa manera de contar. Está escrita, de algún modo, contra la literatura y desconfiado de la literatura. Pero al final, concluí que las personas no somos otra cosa que literatura" (I wrote it, tired of that way of telling a story. It is written, in a sense, against literature and wary of literature. But in the end, I concluded that people are nothing but literature).[5]

Like today's celebrity, the author is constructed so as to be consumed along with his or her product. As Orejudo Utrilla points out in *Fabulosas narraciones por historias*, the image of the author in the consciousness of the reader is but a metaphor. If that is the case, the standard against which the new author is judged in his or her quest for recognition is a fictional one. That standard is in reality a representation of greatness stripped of its human failings, its experience and process of development; it is rather like the busts and other monuments erected in honor of historical and literary figures. The young writer, therefore, does not stand a chance in his or her quest for recognition in this context unless he or she seeks alternative forms of fictionalizing his or her own image. Orejudo Utrilla's Patricio Cordero in *Fabulosas narraciones* has evidently been fooled into mistaking the fictionalized version of the author for the author himself or herself. He therefore attributes his initial failure as a novelist to his lack of a distinguishing feature: "Las famosas vidas ajenas presentaban siempre centenares de marcas. En la suya sin embargo, nunca lograba encontrar ninguna" (The famous lives of others had hundreds of distinguishing features. He could not, however, find any in his life) (11). He envied Proust's tuberculosis, Poe's alcoholism, and the fact that Cervantes had lost an arm. He saw the eccentricities as proof of genius rather than the outcome of a spotlight being shone on the author in the first place. In other words, he did not appreciate the fact that the eccentricity did not make the author, rather it was the author that made the eccentricity. Similarly, W, the "célebre escritor" (famous writer) (65) mentioned earlier in *Ventajas de viajar en tren*, felt that the acquisition of an eccentricity in his sexual tastes was a necessary addition to his fame among his left-wing readership.

From the perspective of both Patricio in *Fabulosas narraciones* and W in *Ventajas de viajar en tren*, their determining characteristics as authors are less related to the written word itself than they are to their personality. The reader is told in *Ventajas de viajar en tren* that the first year after W married Helga Pato, "no escribió ni una línea" (he did not write a single line) (66). However, it appeared as though both he and Helga were in their element. He was sufficiently contented to suggest to the latter that she become his agent. She obliged by creating an agency with the suggestive name of "Imagen y Representación" (Image and Representation) (ibid.), a name that sounds more like that of an agency for film stars and other popular artistes than for authors. Therefore, when she was fired by W and forced to find a way of surviving financially, she had no difficulty in transforming her agency into a commercial enterprise. She began to accept only those authors whose novels allowed her to insert advertisements in them: "Abandonó la literatura de calidad y buscó fórmulas que le permitieran ganar dinero. Y así fue cómo se le ocurrió insertar publicidad en los libros. Pero no en la cubierta, aunque también; ni en la contracubierta, aunque también . . . sino *en* los libros, *dentro* del texto, entretejida a la trama, o separando los capítulos" (she gave up good quality literature and looked for formulas that allowed her to earn money. And that was what led her to insert advertisements in the books. Not only on the cover and the flyleaf . . . but also *in* the books, *inside* the text, intertwined with the plot, or separating the chapters) (68). Meanwhile, she rejected those writings that were inspired in Spain's recent history: "esos melancólicos bodegones sobre la guerra civil, la preguerra civil o la posguerra civil" (those dreary still-life portraits of the civil war, the pre–civil war or the post–civil war period) (ibid.). No matter how "serious" or true to history or how reflexive one considered these civil war–generated novels to be, she saw them as "falsamente reflexivas, que no llegaban a ninguna parte" (falsely reflexive, they went nowhere) (ibid.) because they were not suitable for embedded advertisements.

By revealing the fictional image of Patricio and W as authors, Orejudo Utrilla also reveals that novelists today validate themselves in the same media as popular artistes do. In other words, with the explosion of audiovisual media in the contemporary environment, writers find that they share the same space of authorization as the producers of popular culture. This phenomenon is best illustrated in the transformation of the author into a celebrity. In both of his novels, Orejudo Utrilla turns his self-reflexive fiction onto the ironic and ambivalent relationship between author in the traditional sense and author as celebrity or popular figure. David Lodge provides some insight into the birth of the author as "celebrity." In a review of a biography of Charles Dickens that argues that Dickens may have been "a true celebrity (maybe the first true celebrity in the modern sense)" (quoted in Lodge 2002, 2), Lodge outlines the conditions that make celebrity creation possible: "It requires conditions that did not exist before the Industrial Revolution hit its stride: fast and flexible means of production, transportation, and communication, which circulate the work widely and bring the author into actual or virtual contact with his or her audience" (ibid.).

In *Fabulosas narraciones*, in addition to a central plot about the development of a new literary tradition in the early decades of the twentieth century, the reader also follows the subplot of Patricio's attempt to publish his novel *Los Beatles* and gain some recognition. In the process, he is seen transformed from a novelist who wants to remain independent of trends into one of the abominable literary celebrities. As a celebrity he gives up his attempt to create literature that challenged the literary establishment and rather:

> Construyó, en fin una leve existencia fácil de llevar en privado y un personaje público ciertamente ingenioso, que pasaba por genial entre los incautos, pero que . . . no podía estar expuesto al mismo auditorio más de dos horas seguidas sin riesgo de calcinarse, sin agotar su repertorio de frasecitas y poses. Pero escribir, no escribía ni una línea de calidad. (499)

> [Constructed an easy life that was possible to lead privately and a public personality that was certainly ingenious, which could be passed off as brilliant to gullible people, but which . . . could not be exposed to the same audience for more than two straight hours without the risk of burning out, without exhausting his repertoire of little phrases and poses. But as for writing, he did not write a single line of quality.]

This is not unlike W in *Ventajas de viajar en tren* who simply reveled in his status as a left-wing icon and stopped writing altogether. In the development of the subplot of Patricio's evolution as a novelist, it becomes clear that he is a novelist only in the media. In other words, he has been created by the media. There are two versions of what Patricio is. According to the firsthand information that María Luisa gives Santos, not only did Patricio's first novel *Los Beatles* receive an unfavorable review in *El Sol*, all his subsequent novels were a disaster (419). We get a different picture in the excerpts from the popular magazine *Mujer de Hoy* [Today's woman] that are included in *Fabulosas narraciones por historias*. On each occasion he is described in the popular magazine as "el gran novelista Patricio Cordero Pereda" (the great novelist Patricio Cordero Pereda), and each of the new novels he has just published is described as a "novela llena de belleza, interés, emoción y poesía" (novel filled with beauty, interest, emotion and poetry) (405). Evidently the repetitive nature of the accolades makes the reader suspicious of the supposed value of his works, which have titles like *La Gloria* (405), *Riquezas y Pobrezas*

(Wealth and poverty) (407), *La tentación de la desdicha* (The temptation of misfortune) (415), and *El perseguido* (The fugitive) (475); they sound like titles of popular sentimental fiction. He himself is cognizant of his failure as a "serious novelist" and offers to Santos the following justification of his descent into writing popular fiction:

> En el panorama literario español había dos opciones: o te plegabas a las exigencias editoriales de Ortega y escribías relatos vanguardistas, imaginarios y humorísticos, o no publicabas. Si uno se empeñaba en escribir realismo, debía tener muy claro que ninguna editorial iba a publicar sus libros, a no ser que él mismo se los pagara . . . Él, que no era rico y que había rechazado las ideas de Ortega, se había visto abocado a escribir ese tipo de naturalismo comercial, con mucho sexo implícito a lo Felipe Trigo, que se vendía muy bien. (460)

> [In the Spanish literary scene there were two options: either you bowed to the publishing demands of Ortega and wrote imaginative and humorous avant-garde fiction, or you didn't publish. If one insisted on writing realist fiction, one had to be clear that no publisher was going to publish one's books unless he himself paid for it . . . He, who was not rich and who had rejected the ideas of Ortega, had found himself doomed to write that type of commercial naturalism, with lots of insinuated sex in the style of Felipe Trigo, which sold very well.]

Patricio's position is not unlike that of other writers, some of whom have become accepted into the canon. Indeed, what he goes on to say echoes the idea that celebrity formation is not merely a creation of the contemporary environment and that some of the authors one accepts without question today as established writers have also gone through similar processes of authorization that have not always been literary. He notes further that some of the works of those accepted today were not deemed worthy by their contemporaries in their time:

> Pero él el aprecio o el menosprecio de los intelectuales se lo pasaba por el culo. Clarín había dicho que su tío, el gran Pereda, era un espíritu vulgar y que tenía la misma grandeza y profundidad que un gacetillero. Los intelectuales de la época rechazaron a Fielding cuando éste publicó Tom Jones [*sic*], porque la única intención de aquel libro, dijeron era socavar los cimientos de una moral que padres y educadores estaban obligados a inculcar en las mentes de la juventud. (460–61)

[But as for him, he didn't give a shit about the intellectuals' approval or scorn. Clarín had said that his uncle, the great Pereda, was a vulgar character and that he had the same greatness and depth as a gossip columnist. The intellectuals of the time rejected Fielding when he published *Tom Jones* because the only purpose of that book, they said, was to undermine the morals that parents and educators were obliged to inculcate in the minds of the youth.]

Orejudo's novels show that the alliance between the contemporary writer and the commercial venture of celebrity creation is a rather complex one. He illustrates the conclusion to which Cawelti arrives in the latter's examination of the significance of the creation of literary celebrity in American culture: "In sum, the true celebrity is a human creation of great power and complexity, which approximates in some ways the great mythical figures of ancient times" (174). This complexity is seen not only in Patricio's transformation in Orejudo's novel, but also in the parallel development of a new literary tradition by the group led by the character named after Ortega y Gasset. Beneath the air of seriousness and legitimacy given to the group led by Ortega y Gasset, the narrator reveals a world of crime in which there is no separation between the literati and the rich and fashionable celebrities at the reception held by the Cuevas de Vera family. At the said reception, literary personalities like Ortega y Gasset mingled with the families of General Primo de Rivera and the aristocrats (359–61). Orejudo creates an incongruous, yet plausible, admixture of cultural and literary trends and crime. For example, it turns out that the philanthropic Leo Babenberg not only obtained the money he donated for the promotion of culture through trading in arms, but he also had ulterior motives for being philanthropic:

> Babenberg es un mercader que compra y vende con la misma pasión cañones y poetas, si es que éstos dan dinero. Babenberg les dijo a Ortega, a Juan Ramón Jiménez . . . : tomen este dinero; hagan cuantas Residencias de Estudiantes quieran, pero a cambio multiplíquenme por diez esta cantidad en un plazo equis; yo aumento mi patrimonio y ustedes pasan a la historia. . . . Proyecto: la Generación Poética de los Años Veinte. Prohibido leer novelas; prohibido leer a Galdós; todo el mundo a leer poesía de tuberculosos; si usted quiere ser moderno y estar a la altura de los tiempos, lea literatura vanguardista. (305)

Babenberg is a merchant who buys and sells guns and poets with the same passion, if indeed the latter are profitable. Babenberg said to Ortega and Juan Ramón Jiménez . . . : take this money and build as many Student Hostels as you wish, but in return increase this amount tenfold for me by such and such a date; I will increase my wealth and you will go down in history . . . Project: the Poetic Generation of the Twenties. It is forbidden to read novels; it is forbidden to read Galdós; everyone is required to read the works of consumptive poets; if you want to be modern and to be with the times, read avant-garde literature.]

The revelation of the mercenary side of the generation that is today held in high esteem, as well as the transformation of Patricio into a commercial writer because of his inability to penetrate the closed and controlled arena of established literature, reveals the unhappy but necessary alliance between culture and commerce in contemporary society from the point of view of the new writer. In addition, the mixture of the lowly world of crime and the world of literature makes Orejudo Utrilla's novel, as well as the cultural environment that inspired it, a hybrid of so-called high fiction and low fiction (pornography, popular magazines, tabloid, crime fiction). It is also revealed in the process that the generation that is held in high esteem today was not created in a void. In one of María Luisa's letters to the narrator of *Fabulosas narraciones por historias*, she cautions:

[N]o nos engañemos, lo importante era la cantidad de dinero que movía y generaba un personaje como García Lorca, por ejemplo. Federico llegó a facturar mucho más de lo que gana hoy un tenista profesional. Esta cercanía entre la literatura, el dinero y el poder es lo que hoy prácticamente ha desaparecido. (319)

[Let's not fool ourselves, the important thing is the amount of money that a personality like García Lorca, for example, moved and generated. Federico brought in more than what a professional tennis player earns today. This proximity of literature, money, and power is what is practically disappearing today.]

It is curious that the writer of this letter compares what Lorca, or the character named after Lorca, was worth to what a tennis player earns today. This is yet another attempt at revealing the narrowing gap between popular culture and so-called high culture as a result of the intrusion of market values in all levels of existence. Furthermore, what she claims to have disappeared today—the alliance between money, literature, and power—is untrue. Indeed, one of the charges leveled at literature today is that it is too narrowly linked to market trends and demands.

Orejudo Utrilla's reflexive novels, then, reveal the challenges that authors face in this mercantile context. In *Fabulosas narraciones por historias,* he reveals the flesh-and-blood author behind the fictitious being that is the celebrity or canonized writer. By the time the reader gets exposed to such a writer, he or she has already become a fictional being—a celebrity. Orejudo Utrilla goes behind that fictional image to reveal the person. In the process, he raises pertinent questions about how the "young" writer can become accepted when he or she has to compete with already canonized, and therefore fictional, entities. More importantly, he reveals that the contemporary author shares his or her mode of legitimization with popular cultural products. This is increasingly the case with the media and market explosion in the contemporary environment. This is a further challenge for the "young" writer since, as Orejudo Utrilla suggests, the author's authority is diminished the more he or she operates in the same media of legitimization as do the producers of popular culture.

Having established the diminished authority of the author in contemporary fiction, Orejudo Utrilla brings into focus its significance in relation to the first-person narrative point of view, which is characteristic of Spanish Generation X fiction. In his opinion, the first-person narrative voice smacks of authority that the writers of his generation clearly do not possess. In other words, the subjective perspective that has traditionally suggested and reaffirmed the authority of the voice of the author contradicts the idea of author as artifice. Therefore, whereas most of his contemporaries write themselves out of fictionality by insisting on the first-person narrative point of view and personal experience as raw material for fiction, his objective in *Ventajas de viajar en tren* and *Fabulosas narraciones por historias* is to ridicule the voice of the first-person narrator in order to underline the particular fictionality of contemporary authorship.

In an interview with Luis García posted on Literaturas.com, Orejudo Utrilla explains that he wrote *Ventajas de viajar en tren* because he was "harto de la literatura en general y en particular de la literatura intimista, de ésa que presta mucha atención a los sentimientos, al alma y al ser humano" (fed up with literature in general and in particular with personal narrative, with that kind of literature that pays too much attention to feelings, the soul and the human being). In the same interview he reiterates that his novel "es un alegato contra la literatura intimista, contra la literatura en primera persona" (is an indictment of personal literature, of first-person literature). In an insightful article on the recent trends in Spanish fiction, Orejudo Utrilla discredits the value of the first-person narrator by describing contemporary Spanish fiction as "metonímica o masturbatoria" (metonymic or masturbatory) (2001b, 6). He explains that it is "[m]etonímica porque hace pasar por el todo, por el mundo completo, sólo una parte de él, el YO. Y mastubatorio porque toda la sustancia que extraemos de ella proviene de machacar, o majar . . . esa primera persona" (metonymic because it makes only one part of the world, the I, stand in for the whole world. And it is masturbatory because all the substance that we extract from it is the result of hammering away on that first person) (ibid.).

In *Fabulosas narraciones por historias* Orejudo Utrilla continues the above attempt to expose this fallacy of subjective narrative purporting to be absolute truth. He finds in the "Dear Abby" kind of letters an exaggeration of the first-person narrative focused on the narrator himself or herself. The parody of these letters, addressed to a Dr. Moore who advises readers on personal sexual problems, reflects the masturbatory nature of the narrative that appears to dwell exclusively on the first person. Orejudo Utrilla's rendition of these letters ridicules narratives that focus on the minutiae of a subject's life and dwell on details that may be of interest to no one but the subject itself and may only excite a voyeur. Some of these letters in *Fabulosas narraciones por historias*, however, are all the more ridiculous because they are written as though they would be of interest to the reading public. A few of them begin by explaining that they are writing to Dr. Moore "para hacerle partícipe de mi experiencia y, de paso, algunas consultas" (to share my experience with you and, in passing, consult you) (66). This statement is repeated in at least one other letter: "Me dirijo a usted para hacerle partícipe de mi experiencia y alguna pregunta" (I am writing to you to share my experience with you and to ask you a question) (125). These "preguntas" (questions) arising from the anecdote, which would have given the expert the opportunity to address a problem of universal experience, turn out to be of no consequence. Such is the case of the first of these letters in which the anonymous correspondent claimed to have had sexual intercourse with his mother after she had told him that he was really an adopted child. When his father happens upon them, he joins them in what appears to be a felicitous ménage à trois. His mother admits that she had lied to him (he was really her biological son). On account of this experience, he inquires from Dr. Moore "¿Qué le parece que mi madre me haya mentido? ¿Puedo seguir confiando en ella? ¿Cuál es la mejor postura para la doble penetración? ¿Piensa que la familia es el pilar fundamental de la sociedad?" (What do you think about my mother having lied to me? Can I still trust her? What is the best position for double penetration? Do you think that the family is the fundamental pillar of society?) (128). These questions are irrelevant and absurd and appear to be even more so because of the seriousness with which the so-called expert answers them.

More importantly, these letters are gratifying to the voyeuristic reader, and the publisher of the erotic magazine in which they are published may have exploited them for their commercial value. They appear strategically placed next to advertisements of remedies sold by Dr. Moore for sexually transmitted diseases. In one of the transcriptions of these letters, the advertisement is placed right within the letter itself. No doubt these letters would attract readers like Santos, the confessed consumer of pornography in the novel, to the advertisements considering that some of them are so detailed they read like short pornographic stories. Indeed, Santos confesses to Patricio later on in the novel that he is the author of all the letters that were published in La pasión. While he satisfies his own taste for that sort of narrative by inventing these "Dear Abby" letters of a sexual nature, the publisher of the magazine takes advantage of them to attract readers. This obliges Orejudo Utrilla's own readers to review the value of personal first-person narratives of the kind that are written by some members of his generation. Some of these are so subjective and revealing as to read like reality show scripts. For this reason they risk being dismissed as mere commercial literature in spite of the best intentions of their authors. More importantly, these first-person narrations undermine their fictionality and position themselves inaccurately as voices of authority

Other variations of the supposedly authoritative but subjective first-person texts included in Orejudo Utrilla's *Fabulosas narraciones por historias* are excerpts from biographies, autobiographies, memoirs, interviews, essays, newspaper reports, and minutes of meetings. These excerpts, needless to say, have a more somber tone than the letters sent to Dr. Moore in the popular magazine. Like María Luisa de Babenberg's letters, they also have been included here in this ambiguous work ("Fabulosas narraciones" or "Historias"?) as a means of documenting the cultural environment of the first few decades of the twentieth century in Spain. However, each of these excerpts is flawed. They are all texts that are held to be sacred in one way or the other. However, Orejudo Utrilla manages to discredit them by dislodging them from their position as *the* illustration of reality. He encourages the reader to question their credibility and to view them as just one of many possibilities or fictions. Records of meetings are no doubt considered reliable sources of information as they attempt to record events in text form. In this case it is not the veracity of what is recorded that is at issue. It is rather its content as a textual representation of the cultural environment of the early twentieth century. The minutes of the "Junta de Apoyo a la Juventud y las Artes"; (Organization for the Support of Youth and the Arts) (176) may have been "[t]ranscrito fidedignamente en Madrid, a 4 de noviembre de 1923" (a reliable transcription done in Madrid on November 4, 1923) (181), as is written at the end of them in the novel; however, the contents of the minutes are so ridiculous that they can be challenged by readers: "Por una parte, la Junta estaba consiguiendo acercar la cultura al pueblo sin necesidad de rebajar aquélla, y estaba formando unos ciudadanos siglo veinte que se iban convenciendo de que los folletines de Benito Pérez Galdós constituían lo más truculento que se había escrito en ese país" (On one hand, the Organization was succeeding in bringing culture to the people without needing to lower the standards of the former, and it was creating some twentieth-century citizens who were becoming convinced that Benito Pérez Galdós's serial narratives were the most horrifying things to be written in this country) (176). Similarly, an excerpt, apparently from José Moreno Villa's memoirs, *Vida en claro,* also fails to uphold its credibility due to the nature of the author's selections. The excerpt is so fragmented that the remaining text on its own is absurd and meaningless without the missing context and phrases:

> En el campo se acrecentó mi amor por el aislamiento [. . .]. En la playa conocí el dolor del trabajo [. . .]. No sabré recordar todas las cosas del mar que han contribuido a la formación de mi carácter [. . .]. A los tres meses [de estar en Alemania] hablaba y comprendía las lecciones de la universidad [. . .]. No me gustaban las juergas en mi adolescencia . . . (150)

> [My love for isolation increased in the country [. . .] At the beach I experienced the pain of work [. . .]. I will not be able to remember all that the sea contributed to the formation of my character [. . .]. After three months [of being in Germany] I spoke and I understood the university lectures [. . .]. I did not enjoy living it up when I was a teenager [. . .].][6]

The "authority" implied in all these narratives is undermined in each case to underline the texts' subjectivity.

Orejudo Utrilla therefore criticizes his contemporaries' partiality to the first-person narrative form by comparing that perspective to what he describes elsewhere as "el autoritarismo narrativo en primera persona, que hacia 1600 recibía el nombre de picaresca" (the narrative authoritarianism in the first person, that around 1600 was known as the "picaresque") (2001b, 7). He sums up the significance of the contemporary first-person narrative voice:

> Hay una tendencia muy marcada de la última novela española a construir discursos en primera persona, discursos verbales que no se extienden a lo ancho, sino en vertical, como si no existiera otro universo que el universo individual. Se multiplican así las novelas que ofrecen visiones individuales del universo, voces unívocas, puntos de vista particulares, preocupaciones que quisieran ser universales, pero que no son sino inquietudes pequeñoburguesas. Estas novelas no confrontan estos puntos de vista con otros, opuestos e igualmente reales, se limitan simplemente a no darles cabida en sus universos literarios. Se crea de este modo una especie de dictadura ideológica que borra todo indicio de disidencia, elevando una sola voz individual a la categoría de universal (ibid., 6).

> [There is a very prominent tendency in recent Spanish fiction to construct discourses in the first person, verbal discourses that do not

reach out horizontally but rather vertically, as if no other universe, except the individual one, existed. Thus there is a proliferation of novels that present individual visions of the universe, univocal voices, private points of view, concerns that claim to be universal, but which are only petit bourgeois preoccupations. These novels do not compare these points of view with other points of view, contrasting and equally real; they simply do not allow them a place in their literary universe. In this way a certain ideological dictatorship is created which erases all signs of dissent, elevating only one individual voice to the level of the universal.]

In the same article Orejudo Utrilla says, "Si Cervantes no hubiera confrontado el discurso de *Don Quijote* con ningún otro, hubiera escrito una novela de caballerías más" (If Cervantes had not compared the discourse of *Don Quixote* with another, he would have written another novel of chivalry) (7). Like his mentor Cervantes, then, he maintains an ironic distance from the trend of his time. In addition to ridiculing the overused first-person narrative voice, he chooses to adopt a multiplicity of narrative voices in both *Ventajas de viajar en tren* and *Fabulosas narraciones por historias*. He begins the former with a first-person narrator who immediately undermines his authority by inviting the reader to imagine certain key elements of his story:

Imaginemos a una mujer que al volver a casa sorprende a su marido inspeccionando con un palito su propia mierda. Imaginemos que este hombre no regresa jamás de su ensimismamiento, y que ella tiene que internarlo en una clínica para enfermos mentales al norte del país. Nuestro libro comienza a la mañana siguiente cuando esta mujer regresa en tren a su domicilio. (2000, 11)

[Let's imagine a woman who, on returning home, happens upon her husband inspecting his own shit with a toothpick. Let's imagine that this man never recovers from his state of deep absorption and that she has to have him admitted into a mental health clinic in the North of the country. Our book begins the next morning when this woman is returning home by train.]

Fictionality rather than vital truth appears to be the driving force of *Ventajas de viajar en tren*. As such, the narrator does not take on the univocal stance that it has in novels such as *La conquista del aire* and *Lo real*. Furthermore, the introductory narrator in *Ventajas de viajar en tren* in no way dominates the narrative. The story advances through other characters' monologues and dialogues. Thus the story that is begun by the first-person narrator is almost immediately taken over by a loquacious psychiatrist, Ángel Sanagustín, that the aforementioned woman, Helga Pato, meets on the train. These initial points of view are further increased through the perspectives of the characters in the stories told by Ángel Sanagustín. Several pages later, Ángel Sanagustín's narration is displaced by that of a character in his story, Amelia Urales de Úbeda, who is a former patient's sister. The latter's voice is in the form of a letter that she supposedly sent to Sanagustín. It is not quite certain whether what one reads are really Amelia's words because they are reproduced through Sanagustín, who tells his interlocutor that he remembers "a la perfección" (perfectly) (22). The story that comes out in this letter is itself interspersed with other voices. Interestingly, each new voice is reported by the current narrator, who claims to produce whatever was said "textualmente" (exactly). The other set of significant narrative voices are the first-person introspective narratives of Ángel Sanagustín's patients. Sanagustín claims that he bases his diagnoses on the stories he asks his patients to write (12). Sanagustín left the red folder in which he was carrying some of these stories on the train. Three of them are reproduced in the novel.

Through the multiplicity of narrative voices in *Ventajas de viajar en tren,* "author-ity" is undermined. As a result, the narrative world of the novel is also expanded. It is not only that of the narrator-protagonist easily confused with the author, a situation that results in what Orejudo Utrilla calls "dictadura ideológica" (ideological dictatorship) (2001b, 6). In other words, it is not an individual world. Rather it is a world of a multiplicity of competing individual voices. This is evident in the varying forms of register with their varying sociological and ideological connotations present in *Ventajas de viajar en tren.* Among these voices is that of the narrator, who undercuts the tenets of realism. There is also the impostor, Ángel Sanagustín, who jokingly prefaces his long intervention with the question "¿Le apetece que le cuente mi vida?" (Would you like me to tell you the story of my life?) (11). Ironically, what he goes on to say to Helga Pato discredits subjective narratives. His description of some of the narrative processes involved in the accounts that he solicits from his patients reduces the latter to nothing more than the "mundo de asociaciones [of the patient], que cesa cuando cesa de escribir" (the [patient's] world of associations, which ceases when he ceases to write) (18). In other words, these subjective narratives, emanating from the deep recesses of what other colleagues consider to be the human soul—"la dimensión interior del ser humano" (the interior dimension of the soul) (17)—do not transcend the pathological preoccupation with the self, and they are not really true for all their subjectivity. As examples he refers to the condition of "los coprófilos": "En el caso de los coprófilos todo lo que rodea al paciente pierde valor, los estimulos externos sufren un proceso de devaluación no selectiva, y el paciente queda fascinado por su cuerpo y sus excreciones" (In the case of those who engage in coprophagy, everything around the patient loses its value, the external stimuli go through a process of total devaluation and the patient becomes fascinated by his or her own body and its excretions) (12). The other accounts are those of "los pacientes con esquizofrenia hebefrénica" (patients suffering from hebephrenic schizophrenia) (16). They

> presentan una tendencia no diré irreprimible, pero sí muy marcada a narrar la propia vida. Estos enfermos tienen una particularidad, y lo hacen cada vez de modo diferente, de manera que su personalidad no consiste en otra cosa que una sucesión de relatos superpuestos como las capas de una cebolla. (16)

> [show a marked but not irrepressible tendency to talk about their own lives. These sick people have a special characteristic, and each time they do it differently, such that their personality is nothing more than a succession of superimposed narrations, like the layers of an onion.]

Significantly both conditions referred to are characterized by introspective behavior. People suffering from these conditions are extremely obsessed with themselves to the extent that the "coprófilos" reject any external relationships and the hebephrenics are obsessed with writing only about themselves. Their introspective condition makes their narrative nontranscendental. The reality described by the hebephrenics is appropriately compared to "las capas de una cebolla" (the layers of an onion) (16). Similarly, coprophiliacs' texts only "dan vueltas y vueltas a la misma cosa hasta que al final caen en picado, se estrellan contra su propio pensamiento" (turn the same thing over and over again until finally they fall apart in pieces and explode against their own thoughts) (12). In other words, their texts go nowhere.

W's mental condition, which led Helga to institutionalize him at the "Clínica Internacional," could be considered as a symptom of his self-absorption, which manifests itself in his literary practices. W's state of mind, diagnosed as "trastornos de personalidad" (personality disorder) (93), showed itself in his becoming progressively absorbed in himself. Helga is forced to institutionalize him, however, when upon returning from a trip to the United States she finds him engrossed in the contemplation of his own feces. Obviously he had gone mad. His self-absorption had degenerated into his examination of his own excrement—an extreme case of self-examination to the total exclusion of all else that is outside of the self.

What befell W is not unlike what befell the most famous Spanish fictional character who confused fiction with reality, Cervantes's Don Quixote:

> [É]l se enfrascó tanto en su lectura, que se le pasaban las noches leyendo de claro en claro, . . . y así, del poco dormir y del mucho leer se le secó el cerebro, de manera que vino a perder el juicio. Llenósele la fantasía de todo aquello que leía en los libros, así de encantamentos como de pendencias, batallas, desafíos, heridas, requiebros, amores, tormentas y disparates imposibles; y asentósele de tal modo en la imaginación que era verdad toda aquella máquina de aquellas sonadas invenciones que leía, que para él no había otra historia más cierta en el mundo. (Cervantes 1992, 38)

> [He so buried himself in his books that he spent the night reading from twilight till daybreak, . . . and so from little sleep and much reading, his brain dried up and he lost his wits. He filled his mind with all that he read in them, with enchantments, quarrels, battles, challenges, wounds, wooing, loves, torments and other impossible nonsense; and so deeply did he steep his imagination in the belief that all the fanciful stuff he read was true, that to his mind no history in the world was more authentic.][7]

Don Quixote's madness stemmed from the fact that he transposed a particular kind of fiction—adventures of knights—on the whole of reality. In W's case, he transferred to the realm of fiction a reductive reality—the self. Thus he abandons the bigger world out there and closes in on himself. This is the meaning of his examination of his own waste.

What sets Orejudo Utrilla's narrative style apart from that of his contemporaries is not only his use of multiple narrators, but more importantly that the "truth" of each one of those threads in the story is undermined. The narrator of *Ventajas de viajar en tren*, as mentioned before, underscores the fictionality of his story by prefacing his interventions with "imaginemos" (let's imagine). The stories of his characters are also thrown into question when it becomes clear that their authenticity is questionable. For example, Amelia Urales Úbeda turns out to be her brother Martín Urales Úbeda. It later turns out too that Dr. Ángel Sanagustín is not a psychiatrist as he had claimed but rather Martín Urales Úbeda impersonating his brother-in-law. The other stories are written by psychiatric patients, a fact that undermines their veracity. It would appear that Helga Pato is the only "real" character standing. But one cannot be sure of that since the novel ends with her meeting Martín Urales Úbeda on a train once again after the latter was supposed to have died in a fire. It leaves one wondering which of the two characters is an invention of the other. Impersonators, schizophrenic narrators, and fictional narrators, when juxtaposed against the first-person introspective narrator typical of Generation X fiction, throw into question the reliability of the latter and reveal its contradiction of the postmodern individual who is unstable, fragmented, incoherent, and inconsistent in a context of multiple voices and truths.

The characters of Orejudo Utrilla's first novel are similarly unreliable as they attempt to pass off their "Fabulosas narraciones" as "historias," hence the title of the novel: *Fabulosas narraciones por historias*. As in the case in *Ventajas de viajar en tren*, no one voice dominates the text. In fact, the third-person narrative voice with which Orejudo Utrilla begins the novel is soon confused with that of the character about whom he writes. In the process of informing the reader about the character's anxieties as a novelist (the character turns out to be Patricio), he transcribes in a following paragraph the latter's very thoughts in the first person: "[E]n fin, siempre estoy a tiempo de ser un mal escritor, denominarme novelista singular, como Unamuno, y llegar a figura señera de las letras españolas" (Anyway, I am still in time to become a bad writer, to call myself a singular novelist, like Unamuno, and to become a key figure in Spanish letters) (14). With no further transition the text switches back to the third-person narrator, "[a] punto estaba precisamente de quedarse dormido aquella noche, agotado de buscarse marcas por todo el cuerpo" (he was, precisely, about to fall asleep that night, exhausted from searching for marks all over his body) (14–15), leaving the reader wondering who is telling the story. This ambivalent point of view at the beginning of the novel, one soon realizes, is characteristic of the rest of the novel in various forms that undermine, rather than justify, the authority of the subjective narration. As with *Ventajas de viajar en tren*, not even one of the points of view that contribute to this novel can be accepted as credible.

One of the significant competing voices in *Fabulosas narraciones por historias* is that of María Luisa de Babenberg. Her letters appear to have all the credibility one attributes to the epistle, and they are ostensibly the source of historical information that the writer of the novel (the reader finds out later) intends to use as material for his writing. There is no reason to doubt the veracity of the first letter, for example, in which she writes of the most mundane of her memories of Madrid in the twenties: "Madrid, años veinte, a las diez de la mañana, es una pescadería estrecha con el mostrador inclinado hacia la calle, que da gloria verlo con sus merluzas, sus pescadillas, su salmón fresco y su atún, sus sardinas" (Madrid, 1920s, at ten in the morning, is a narrow fish shop with a counter tilted toward the street; it is delightful to see it with its hake, its fresh salmon, its tuna, its sardines) (16–17). It is a very subjective representation of Madrid from her point of view; hardly the type of description that would have been given by any other person who lived there at the time. It is all the more apparently credible because of its subjectivity; after all, she had actually, it would appear, experienced the city as such. Ironically, however, in her own letters she points out that she is suspicious of other first-person narratives, such as the memoirs that she claimed had become fashionable among her contemporaries. Of the memoirs she says:

Cada libro ha sido una sorpresa mayor y una confusión más grande. ¡Si parecía que habíamos vivido vidas diferentes en mundos distintos y épocas lejanas unas de las otras! Muchos de estos libros relatan sucesos que yo presencié y en los que tuve un cierto protagonismo. Pues bien, tras la lectura de ese centenar de testimonios aclaradores, ni yo sé a ciencia cierta qué ocurrió. (233)

[Each book has been a big surprise and caused great confusion. It looked as if we had lived different lives, in different worlds and in periods that were far apart from each other! Many of these books related events that I witnessed and in which I had played an important role. Well, after reading those hundreds of elucidating accounts, even I don't know for certain what happened.]

One could make the same comment about the contents of her letters. Her version of certain events does not coincide with other versions of the same events in the novel. In addition, in the last letter included in the novel, she alleges that her co-correspondent "[h]a incluido cartas que [ella] no [ha] escrito y ha modificado las verdaderas hasta dejarlas irreconocible" (has included some letters that [she] did not write and has modified the real ones so much that they are unrecognizable) (513). Considering the modifications that the passage of time and her own choices had inflicted on her memory as well as the "author's" own modifications, one is left with a text that is no more reliable than any other in the novel.

In both Orejudo Utrilla's novels he reveals the representational nature of the notion of author. Consequently, he suggests that the proliferation of first-person narratives, with their suggestion of authors imposing their perspective as if they held the key to the ultimate truth, failed to reflect the diminished power of the author. According to his two novels, the media through which the author and his work are legitimized are common to other representations in popular culture. This is so, especially, in the contemporary period dominated by market demands and audiovisual media. Orejudo Utrilla then seems to be aware of the fact that the novel that one has in hand is a product of several factors that are not necessarily literary. In this context and in the context of plural and varying media of communication, plural points of view, varying points of tension and concerns in the contemporary world, Orejudo Utrilla reveals the "young" writer's anxiety around his or her authority. Since the author and his or her work are creations dependent on practices outside of the literary, and since those practices are shared by popular forms of representation, the former are taken down from the pedestal of cultural expression and shown to be competing with popular voices and media in Orejudo Utrilla's novels. The author in this contemporary context then, loses his or her sacred voice of authority. Furthermore, Orejudo Utrilla shows that the author as "authority" is undermined by the proliferation of other media of expression, as the written word is no longer the central source of knowledge and truth. Orejudo Utrilla seems to suggest through his two novels that fiction be accepted for what it is: representation. To ignore the undeniable role that extraliterary forces play in the creation of fiction and in manipulating the image of its authors is to deny this fundamental characteristic of fictional literature.

Conclusion

THE SPANISH GENERATION X WRITERS' PREOCCUPATION WITH IDENTI-
ties that are weakened rather than affirmed in this media-dominated and market-driven globalized environment is evident in
various manifestations of the following in their novels: the recurrent image of solitary and alienated characters; the repeated theme
of such characters' entrapment in a present that does not appear
to be related to a past; the unstable location of the novelists'
fiction between high and low cultures; and their condition in a
globalized, postcapitalist world. In addition, the general literary
instability of this period is expressed through an element of self-
reflexiveness in each of these novels. Given these characteristics,
one can describe these Spanish Generation X novelists and their
contemporaries as a generation of solitary subjects; a generation
of the here and now; a generation caught in between high and low
cultures; a postcapitalist and self-reflexive generation.

A GENERATION OF SOLITARY SUBJECTS

The most recurrent image in these Generation X novels is that
of the solitary and alienated subject. In *Historias del Kronen,* for
example, the central character, Carlos, displays a remarkable inability to connect with other people. Similar demonstrations of
this antisocial behavior have been described as a contemporary
failing in human relations and have been attributed by Robert
Dunn to "a rapidly changing landscape of capitalist consumerism
and the evolving means of signification constituting mass culture
and informational society" (1998, 64). In the case of Carlos, he is
so overrepresented in his first-person musings on the minutiae of
his life that the "other" is acutely absent:

> Termino de desayunar y salgo a la piscina. Me tumbo al sol, me pongo
> los cascos y duermo un poco. Luego me hago un par de largos, me

seco, entro de nuevo en casa y le pregunto a la filipina si ha llamado
alguien mientras he estado en la piscina. (38)

[I finish having breakfast and go out to the swimming pool. I lie down
in the sun, put on my earphones, and nap a little. Then I do a couple
of laps, dry myself, go back into the house, and ask the Filipino woman
if anyone called while I was in the pool.]

Carlos's inability to process a concept of an "other" shows itself in
his egoistic introversion. For this he is harshly reprimanded by one
of his friends who reminds him that "[t]ú no eres nada sin los
demás. Es lo primero de lo que te das cuenta cuando maduras"
(you are nothing without other people. It is the first thing you realize when you become mature) (170). Indeed, Carlos's carnivales-
que excessive exhibition of an unpredictable self to the exclusion
of family members and friends appears to thrive only within the
spaces inhabited by privately consumed media images but lacks
the permanence afforded by social interaction. Consequently, as
the novel progresses, he appears to be threatened with annihila-
tion in spite of his paradoxical excessive presence.

Like *Historias del Kronen*, Belén Gopegui's novels are urban in
focus and deal with the sense of loneliness, instability, and insecurity arising from the realization that one's assumptions and pre-
conceptions regarding one's self are no longer sustainable in an
economically and culturally porous environment. The troubled
characters of Gopegui's novels appear to suffer from an identity
crisis arising from the tension between self-determination through
traditional associations of family, work, ideology, and a relationship to others on one hand and self-determination through acts of
consumption or a relationship to things on the other.

The middle-class characters in *La conquista del aire* and *Lo
real*, having previously acted against absorption by "large-scale
entities such as the bureaucracy, the state, the factory, the market
and mass society" (Dunn 1998, 55), had assumed identities based
on a preconception of self-unity, consistency, coherence, and stability, as well as the possession of autonomy. All this begins to
crumble as they are absorbed one by one into the value system of
the market and are alienated from peers and family members with
whom they had shared socialist ideals. The recurrent sense of isolation of the subject and the concomitant feeling of loss of auton-

omy are echoed in *La conquista del aire* in the thoughts of the narrator as the characters lay sleeping, individually, each alone with his or her thoughts: "Duermen. La política no está. La facultad de elegir qué criterios ordenarán la existencia se ha perdido. La democracia comercial y comunicativa es un estanque" (They are sleeping. Politics is absent. The ability to choose the criteria that will determine existence is lost. Commercial and communicative democracy is only a still pond) (340).

These same thoughts resonate throughout the rest of the novels studied here as the various characters appear to be trapped and isolated rather than liberated in the supposedly democratizing market and informational environment. For example, the alienating effect of capitalism on identity is particularly evident in Ismael Grasa's *De Madrid al cielo*. Grasa's protagonist, Zenón, is like the subject described by Moreiras Menor as the "abject subject, dispossessed of identity, [who] wanders without a trace" (2000, 139), due to the erosion of certain referents of identity formation such as family, labor, and political affiliations in the aftermath of Spain's vertiginous integration into the market and consumer economy. His existential malaise resonates in his words "nadie me reconoce ahora por mi trabajo; . . . Las cosas son así, cuesta abajo" (no one recognizes me anymore for my work . . . That is how things are, downhill) (29–30). These are the words of a man who has gone from being a busker with socialist leanings to becoming an almost homeless ragman in a society with no tolerance for the likes of him.

THE GENERATION OF THE HERE AND NOW

The existential malaise and the isolation experienced by the characters in these novels are also attributable to, and evident in, the idea that they are caught in a present that is overrepresented to the exclusion of history. Within the so-called free market, globalized, and technologically mediated environment, which is referred to as "la democracia comercial y comunicativa" by Gopegui's narrator in *La conquista del aire* (338), the privileging of the present displaces the subject further, for identity itself tends to be rooted in history.

It is suggested that the environment within which Gopegui's

characters operate in *La conquista del aire*, for example, fright-fully appears to be chronologically closed in on itself:

> [E]n la democracia comunicativa no hay desdicha, cualquier interfe-rencia viaja al espacio exterior por los áureos canales y no hay muerte, no hay tiempo sino un circuito que cada año se repite; el antes no pre-cede al después sino que son intercambiables y sólo en el abismo la luz no es uniforme. (337–38)

> [There is no misfortune in the communicative democracy; any inter-ference travels to outer space through the golden channels; there is no death; there is no time but rather a circuit that is repeated every year; the before does not precede the after, but rather both are interchange-able, and it is only in the abyss that the light is not uniform.]

"La democracia comercial y comunicativa" erases history, as Santiago, one of Gopegui's characters, intuits when he has four million pesetas saved up in his account. The democratizing effect of the money completely dissociates him from his past. With the money in his account, he happily realizes that "yo no fui un don nadie, . . . sino un hombre cualquiera, una cuenta corriente cual-quiera que se unía a la cuenta de Leticia Tineo" (I was not a no-body . . . but rather just any man with a checking account which was joined to that of Leticia Tineo) (338). His past, like history, is confined to what the narrator of *La conquista del aire* calls "el abismo" where human tragedy, war, pain, and the like are con-tained.

A similar displacement of the past by the present is evident in Mañas's novel as well. *Historias del Kronen* is obviously located in a significant historical period: 1992; this fact is not lost on the reader because of the frequent allusions to the 1992 Olympic Games held in Barcelona. There are several other references to news items of national and international importance, such as nine Polish immigrants who die in a fire in Móstoles, the war in Yugo-slavia, and truck drivers on strike in France (100). Curiously, these events do not seem to have any impact on the narrator; Car-los appears to be caught in the eternal present, except for when he complains about the lack of elements of entertainment in the news. In the news, at least from his perspective, history/reality is indistinguishable from entertainment.

Carlos's relationship to history confirms the observation that, "the reason why postmodernism has been seen as an 'end of history' is its stress on representation, reflecting the 'death of the real' produced by mass media conversion of reality into images and its replacement in information technology by simulated models" (Labanyi 1995a, 399). Carlos's preoccupation with representation or entertainment rather than history locks him into an eternal present. The only moment in which history or reality rears its head is when Miguel, one of his friends, brings up the question of racism, youth unemployment, and the threat to "Spanishness" with the country's integration into the European Union. Miguel cautions his friends who are caught in the spectacle of the present: "No te rías, Celia. Si es que todo está muy mal. Mucha Expo y mucha olimpiada pero en Madrid no hay dinero" (Don't laugh, Celia. Things are really going badly. There is a lot about Expo and the Olympics, but in Madrid there is no money) (205). Carlos unfortunately is oblivious to this reality and this contributes to and reflects his alienation from those around him.

In *De Madrid al cielo,* the efforts of the protagonist, Zenón, to make meaning out of the present is related to an attempt to retrieve an elusive past. However, these are fruitless efforts that increase his sense of dislocation. Significantly, Zenón's surroundings—the city of Madrid—which should embody history and "Spanish otherness," and therefore provide him with references for identification, fail to do so. This is because the Spanish capital in Grasa's novel is not rooted in history but rather in representation or in spectacle. Madrid, the sign of "Spanishness," exists only in print media, in August, for example, when Pirulo, the veteran vendor of sunflower seeds at Retiro Park, is photographed for the local newspaper. As Zenón observes, Pirulo appears in the papers as a symbol of Madrid "provinciana" (37). That image is, however, only a media invention, because Pirulo does not really sell much in terms of traditional Spanish snacks. What he really sells are "chicles con azúcar y sin azúcar, chocolatinas, gominolas, gusanitos, y así" (regular and sugarless chewing gum, chocolate bars, gummy bears, candy worms, and such) (ibid.). In other words, he sells the same wares as one would find on the tray of a vendor in any other modern consumer society. Spanishness, history, or the image of Madrid as a traditional city is located, then, in the media, in the same place as the representations of the West that Zenón sees in the popular magazines: photographs of Marilyn Monroe, Katherine Hepburn and Audrey Hepburn (52).

In Gabriela Bustelo's *Veo veo* time seems to stand still as, "los noctambuleros seguían ensayando una y mil veces las mismas escenas insulsas de una anquilosada obra de teatro que nadie quería dirigir" (the night-birds continued to rehearse for the thousandth time the same insipid scenes of an outdated play that no one wanted to direct) (20). The world described by the narrator is that of the superficial middle class trapped in the cult of designer and consumer culture that, once again, is only sustainable in the present of the spectacle.

In all of these novels, access to capital or to the audiovisual media's ability to construct reality and image result in the separation of some of the characters from the past or from reality. This contributes to the recurrent image of subjects who seem to be disconnected from one another and also from the environment in which they live. As a consequence, and contrary to expectation, they are unable to wield control over their destiny.

A Generation in a Global Encounter

The context in which Spanish Generation X novelists write and the preoccupations inspired by that context places them in a transnational rather than a national framework. This then raises questions around the autonomy or particularity of contemporary Spanish literature versus the subordination of Spanish cultural expression to a dominant center within the globalized culture. After all, as Ryszard M. Machnikowski has pointed out, "global culture is primarily a culture of U.S.–dominated elites. . . . As far as culture is concerned, globalization means Americanization" (2000, 94). This impression would appear to be confirmed through the portrayal of characters such as Ismael Grasa's Zenón, who is like a character out of detective fiction or film noir and who is obsessed with some of the icons of North American popular culture, especially Marilyn Monroe. Once when he was going to sell a pile of old books and papers that included "un ejemplar censurado del *Quijote* con ilustraciones de Doré" (a censored copy of the *Quijote* with illustrations by Doré) (52), he was more willing to part with the latter than sell "un libro ilustrado de actrices norteamericanas" (an illustrated book of North American actresses) that included "doce fotografías de Marilyn" (twelve photographs of Marilyn) (ibid.).

Like *De Madrid al cielo,* other novels such as *La pistola de mi hermano* and *Veo veo* can be seen as imitations of master narratives of popular Hollywood genres and therefore dismissed as evidence of the "Americanization" of these narratives. However, that would only be mere simplification, less than half of the story told. In fact, Spanish Generation X writers react to rather than mimic Western economic and cultural practices by revealing the tension between their subjects and the Western practices apparently upheld in their novels.

Indeed, Spanish critic Gonzalo Navajas dismisses claims of the homogenizing effect of a U.S.–dominated global culture on contemporary Spanish literature and film. He attributes what he considers to be a combination of nationalism and globalism in contemporary Spanish literature and film to the latter's integration into "el paradigma internacional" (the international paradigm) in which

> [lo] nacional ha dejado de ser estrictamente local . . . para asumir presupuestos del discurso internacional: el replanteamiento de los cánones culturales, la irrupción de los medios audiovisuales frente al lenguaje de la cultura clásica, el predominio del entretenimiento sobre la reflexión, los nuevos temas del *hic nunc* asociados sobre todo con la juventud (individualidad, deflación ética colectiva, gratificación inmediata, celeridad vital) en vez de los grandes conceptos de la inmanencia histórica cultural. (2002, 184–85)

> [what is national is no longer strictly local . . . it takes on assumptions from international discourse: the reconsideration of the cultural canons, audiovisual media explosion versus the language of classical culture, the predominance of entertainment over reflection, the new themes of the here and now associated especially with youth (individuality, collective ethical deflation, immediate gratification, vital velocity) instead of the grand concepts of historical cultural immanence.]

For Navajas, then, the very discourse that would be dismissed as a sign of the encroachment of American-dominated popular cultural practices on Spanish Generation X fiction is evidence of a creative encounter between the national and the global culture. He, however, disregards the power play that is inevitable in such an encounter.

Moreiras Menor, however, is cognizant of the hegemonic power of American-dominated cultural practices when it comes to the fiction by this generation of writers considered to be "una de las manifestaciones singulares de la internacionalización de la cultura española de los noventa" (one of the singular manifestations of the internationalization of Spanish culture in the nineties) (Urioste 1997–98, 456). In Moreiras Menor's opinion, the result of this global encounter is trauma expressed in contemporary fiction and film through the immersion of the subject into a culture of spectacle and a preoccupation with violence. She describes Spanish culture at the intersection of the global and the national as "a wounded culture, a culture in shock" (2000, 137) whose subject "is dispossessed of will-power and . . . is lost amid the violence generated by the erosion of the state which coincided in Spain with the dawn of the society of spectacle and of the market-place" (138). This is most accurately demonstrated in the self-destructive preoccupation with violence that is evident in novels like *La pistola de mi hermano* and *Historias del Kronen*. It is subtle but present, nevertheless, in the other novels, such as *La conquista del aire*, in which the characters find themselves torn away from the relationships and associations with which they had been accustomed in the older political and social order.

THE GENERATION OF HYBRID CULTURES: IN BETWEEN THE HIGH AND THE LOW

Spanish Generation X fiction is also located in the contested boundary between high and low culture. Some of the novels in this study are manifestations of Fredric Jameson's often repeated description of the postmodern condition characterized by the "effacement [in them] of some key boundaries or separations, most notably the erosion of the older distinctions between high culture and so-called mass popular culture" (1991, 112). In Spanish fiction, popular culture has always played a pivotal role in the tensions between authoritarian structures and material and cultural liberalization. The high incidence of popular forms in Spanish fiction since the mid-twentieth century can be attributed to the shift away from "master discourses" and "totalizing representations" (Spires 1996, 28) that parallel the norms of authoritarian social and political structures. The high incidence of mass culture in contemporary Spanish fiction, and in Generation X fiction in particular, features as a sign of Spain's integration into and participation in a modern political and economic order that had eluded novelists who wrote under authoritarian regimes. What makes today's fiction different from previous ones with regard to the fusion of high and popular culture in literature, however, is the general absence in the former of a confrontation with political authoritarianism and an involvement, rather, with the impact of economic and technological totalitarianism on the production and distribution of culture.

Furthermore, the blurring of the barriers between high and low culture in Spanish Generation X fictions can therefore be attributed to the expansion of the medium of expression and cognition from the typographic, in which literature has been conventionally expressed, to include audiovisual media as well. Audiovisual communication has traditionally been the vehicle of expression for private, as opposed to collective, experience, and entertainment, as opposed to reflective thought. One of the most important factors that differentiate some of these novelists from the established generation of writers is their bold displacement of the hegemony of typographical language and the incorporation in their work of forms of expressions associated with television, film, and computers. In Spanish Generation X novels one finds a situation similar to the one described by Manuel Castells in which literature loses its place of authority as writers participate in the new communicative system and way of thinking that incorporates a multiplicity of communicative modes, including audiovisual media, in self-expression. According to Castells, "text" thus loses its superior status as it shares its space in cultural expressions with popular forms such as talk shows, reality TV, rock music, and fashion. However, these writers do not merely provide an illustration of what their reality is with regard to audiovisual media of communication. In appearing to portray its high incidence in contemporary day-to-day life, they also analyze the impact of audiovisual communication on their vision of the world and of themselves.

In addition, in Spanish Generation X fiction, the questioning of the hierarchical opposition between high and low culture is also reflected in a concern with the tension between audiovisual and textual culture. This leads to a further problematization of reality and its relationship to representation in the works in this study. Within a communicative environment, appropriately described as "multisensorial" as opposed to predominantly typographic by Castells (1996, 373), "representation" through audiovisual media threatens to replace the experience itself. This is demonstrated in *Veo veo,* for example, in which virtual reality in the form of cinematic fiction and its characters attempt to take over the real life of the central character. Spanish Generation X novelists reflect, not so much the overpowering nature of reality ("people's material and symbolic existence" [ibid.])by the medium, but rather that situation in which, as Robert Dunn puts it, "signifier and referent invade each other's realms, threatening the distinction between the real and its representation" (1998, 100).

Spanish Generation X writers are not only preoccupied with the fact that the "staging" (Dunn 1998, 101) of reality is threatening reality itself, but are also concerned with the economic, social, political, and cultural imperatives behind the representation, as well as the subject's place and autonomy within a represented world in which agency is undermined or modified. The question is, how do "young" writers, such as those in this generation, attain recognition and acceptance when literary norms are being challenged by the evolution of expression, production, and distribution? This is the question that in one way or another informs many of the novels published by this generation in the last decade. It is evident in the self-conscious blurring of the traditional barriers between so-called high and low culture in novels like Ismael Grasa's *De Madrid al cielo,* in which the author relies on narrative strategies and structures typical of popular culture. The same question can also be found in the underlying tension between what is considered to be literature and what is not in Belén Gopegui's prologue to *La conquista del aire.*

THE POSTCAPITALIST GENERATION

The above discussion leads directly to another aspect of the breaking down of barriers in Spanish Generation X fiction: the interpenetration of aesthetic obligations and the demands of commodity production and distribution. Spanish Generation X fiction needs to be considered within the context of the dynamics of Spain's place in the contemporary globalized consumer society. In this regard, one needs to take into account not only the direct allusions made in some of these novels to commodity culture, but also how the latter impinges on the production and distribution of literature in general. In the past few decades, beginning in the waning years of Francoism, Spain has witnessed a dizzying descent into the realms of globalized commodity culture. In a relatively short period, compared to other European countries and the United States, Spain has emerged from the grips of Francoist economic and cultural autarky, becoming fully immersed in the globalized consumer economy. Enrique Bustamante's description of the Spanish cultural industry in the 1990s underlines the replacement of national capital with foreign interests which undercut any form of cultural policy or social protest. In various cultural sectors, such as the publishing industry, the record industry, cinema, video, and advertising, a few multinational groups control more than 50 percent of sales (1995, 360). Traditionally, post-Franco Spanish fiction has been read within the context of the effects of the political dictatorship; it is now appropriate to read it in the context of dominating market forces. In doing so, one better appreciates the tightrope that the contemporary writer walks between canonical literary conventions and the demands of the process of distribution of culture.

This period of Spanish Generation X literature is best described as a period in flux, a period of uncertainties that are evident in the debates and the criticisms generated by the idea of a Generation X group of writers. The factors contributing to the destabilization of the secure notion of what Spanish fiction should be in the minds of most critics, writers, and cultural commentators include the following, which are interrelated: the unavoidable role of market practices and communication media in the production and distribution of literature.

The market and technological demands and possibilities have contributed to blurring the boundaries between commercial and entertainment literature and so-called serious literature or between literature and commerce in general. It is not uncommon today for a novelist to have a personal Web site in which to promote himself or herself as well as his or her work. Consequently, he or she is able to reach a wide public, not only via the actual text of his or her work but also through extraliterary media such as his or her personality or physical appearance. This is made possible with easy and accessible audiovisual media that have long been exploited by other artistes such as singers and actors.

Similarly, literary award ceremonies today can be highly publicized affairs not unlike award ceremonies in popular culture, and their focus is not only on the text in question but also on the image of the writer. In the contemporary environment image acquires a significance never before experienced in literary culture, as one was made to appreciate in the much-publicized affair of the red dress that Lucía Etxebarria wore to the Nadal award ceremony in 1998. The media's response to the controversial attire shows that the author also plays the role of protagonist in the cultural environment. The transformation of the author into protagonist is not new. What is new is the extent and power of the current media of communication. This contributes to separating the writer even more from the written word. By focusing on the extraliterary elements, the media feeds the notion that its literary favorites definitely lack in literary value.

The impact of twenty-first-century communication media on the production and distribution of literature is similar to the effect that newspapers had on the nineteenth-century novelist. In the nineteenth century, when the development of continuous rolls of paper, the steam-powered press, and iron presses made printing more efficient and cheaper, the newspapers took on an even bigger role in the promotion of authors. The papers became significant as avenues for giving exposure to authors and their books. Much has already been written about the promotional value of the trend of serialized fiction in nineteenth-century newspapers. Critics have pointed out the promotional tactic of publishers encouraging authors to participate in the current cultural and political polemics in newspapers to boost the sale of their own works. "It would be a mistake," points out John Cawelti

> to assume that celebrity is a problem utterly unique to modern times. The artist as person-performer and therefore, to some degree, as celebrity has been a factor since the dawn of literature. Certainly those wandering bards whose tradition led to the great epics of Homer had a kind of celebrity. One can easily imagine a village crowd gathered around

one of Homer's grandfathers eagerly questioning him about his work, just as reporters cluster around one of today's literary celebrities. (1977, 164)

The most significant difference between celebrity creation in the past and in contemporary circumstances, quite apart from the extent of the practice, is that in previous cases the process took place within the same medium as the works in question. In other words, the bards attained celebrity status by word of mouth, and similarly, the nineteenth-century novelist promoted himself by means of his own writing in the growing newspaper industry. Today, however, the skills required for the writers' promotion do not appear to have anything to do with his or her own ability as a writer. They are skills and functions that have already been honed by actors in popular genres and that have become associated with them. It is common now to find writers sharing the spotlight in newspapers and on the Internet, for example, with other products. Novels are promoted in the same space as summer travel deals. The Internet, on which some novelists have their personal Web sites, like their counterparts in the popular music industry, allows the former to create a "fan" base and sell more books in the same way as musicians would sell records. The use of the television, newspapers, and magazines to promote the writer makes the person, rather than his or her work or the text, significant.

The questions in some of the interviews of writers published in these media, especially on the Internet, are not unlike those that fans ask popular artistes based on the received image or the image that they would like to form of them. Indeed, one is reminded of these "fan" interviews that focus of the image of a writer by the questions that a young girl asks Santos of Patricio in *Fabulosas narraciones por historias:*

> Santos se vio en la tesitura de tener que describir a Patricio. Ella quería saberlo todo de él: qué le gustaba hacer, qué era lo que más detestaba en el ser humano, sus creencias religiosas, cuál era su cualidad favorita en los hombres, con qué personaje histórico le gustaría celebrar una cena íntima, cuál era la virtud que mejor apreciaba en la mujer hoy. (399–400)

> [Santos found himself in the situation of having to describe Patricio. She wanted to know all about him: what he liked to do, what he hated

most in human beings, his religious beliefs, what his favorite human quality was, the historical personality that he would most like to have an intimate dinner with, the virtue that he most admired in women today.]

The phenomenon described above is not new. However, it is the writer at the end of the twentieth century, like Antonio Orejudo Utrilla and his contemporaries, who are most concerned about its implications with respect to their status and their authority as writers. Since it borrows its strategies and processes of authorization from the area of popular culture, their literature tends to be dismissed as commercial and therefore unserious fiction.

THE METAFICTIONAL MODE AND THE "INSECURE" AUTHOR

On the whole, the questions, tensions, and contradictions surrounding the nature of fiction tend to manifest themselves in the proliferation of self-reflexive narratives, and this is one of the defining characteristics of Spanish Generation X fiction. Many novelists in this generation draw attention to their fiction as artifacts in the process of being created. In doing so they blur the lines between reality and fiction, as both author and his or her work penetrate the created fictional world they are in the process of creating or become its focus. The proliferation of metafictional narratives in Spanish Generation X fiction may be considered as a reaction to the breakdown of various systems of language, society, culture, and identity.

As Patricia Waugh explains in her study of this literary phenomenon, metafiction is spawned by the "uncertain, insecure, self-questioning and culturally pluralistic" (1984, 6) historical period in which we live. This is especially true for Generation X novelists writing as they are in the unstable environment of world culture and writing at the end of the second millennium in a rapidly changing environment that calls into question fundamental issues around just about every aspect of human experience. On a national level the authors in question have, like the rest of the Spanish population, in the last decade experienced the destabilizing impact of major social, cultural, political, and economic transformations on their identity. For example, they have experienced firsthand the impact of massive youth unemployment or underemployment and the challenge posed by globalization, as well the explosion of audiovisual and network communications media to their Spanish national identity. These authors, as we have seen in the preceding chapters, are confronted with a changing landscape of several facets of contemporary life, and they have to find meaning within it. In their literary expression, therefore, they are preoccupied with the inadequacy of the conventions of writing to reflect their vision of the world and what constitutes acceptable literature.

Consequently, their fiction tends to illustrate the tensions between competing modes of representation, media of expression, and genres. In the process of challenging the certainties implied in the conventional forms of representation, they also explore the uncertainties of their own existence, an issue at the core of most Spanish Generation X writing. The young writer's questions about his/her legitimacy as author can also be gleaned from Gabriela Bustelo's deauthorization of her first-person narrative voice in a context in which real and media (television/film) spaces are confused. It is as though the Spanish Generation X writers' search for adequate themes and modes of expression is paralleled by an equally intense search for self. This, in my opinion, explains why the self-conscious fictions of this generation also privilege the first-person point of view of narration. In these, narrator, protagonist, and author appear to be confused, such as in the novels by José Ángel Mañas and Ray Loriga examined in this study.

Metafictional narratives reveal not only the hand behind fiction creation but also speak to "contemporary experience of the world as a construction, an artifice" (Waugh 1984, 9). In revealing the artifice behind fiction, the writer is obliged to reveal the fictionalizing effect of all modes of representation, even of those that purport to represent the "truth," such as the news and other television programs. This is the general preoccupation of the narrator in Loriga's *La pistola de mi hermano*, in which the former's perspective on his brother's crime is developed alongside that of its television version in the news and talk shows. The extreme fictionalizing effect of representation and the professional management of (real) news in the "Network Age" are all too familiar to the young narrator who recalls the reduction of the Gulf War to nothing but "simulacra": "Como cuando los americanos bombardearon Iraq y todo lo que se veía era un montón de colores, sin muertos, ni nada" (similar to when the Americans bombed Iraq and all that could be seen were a bunch of colors, without dead people or anything) (121).

As they draw attention to other forms of representation as contested reality, Generation X writers are confronted with a dilemma centering on themselves: their own reality becomes questionable, and thus they become anxious about their own existence as authors. These novels are therefore characterized by an anxiety surrounding the self, because the authors as "creators" are all too aware of their vulnerability to the processes of representation in other communication media.

Revealing the "artificial" nature of fictional narratives also leaves the author vulnerable. He or she becomes insecure, destabilized, and uncertain. In the process of the self-conscious narrator peeling away the trappings that give representations the illusion of the real, the "fictional" image of the "lone creative figure busily inventing and constructing, producing the text from His [*sic*] position in the Real World" (Waugh 1984, 130) also becomes open to question. For the "author," before he or she becomes known to his or her readership as such, has also gone through a process of constructions and fabrications to arrive at attaining that designation. The real and therefore unstable and insecure entity before its representation as "author" is revealed in some of the novels reviewed so far through self-conscious writers shown up for being humanly fallible, unreliable, and manipulative. Some of the fictional writers are even shown up for being social failures who are struggling in their work or who are reworking their texts, and who inhabit a world that they cannot confirm to be "real" after all.

In one way or another, each of the novels dealt with in this book reflects Generation X novelists' engagement with agency diminished by the power of the media and/or the market. Some of their characters' individual tastes and consuming habits are fueled by consumerism to the detriment of solidarity with others. Their subjects' perception of reality is manipulated by, and distorted through, media representation. Furthermore, in the media-dominated environment of these novels, the past, in which identity should be anchored, is displaced by an eternal present. Thus, the subjects of Generation X fiction find themselves unmoored in an ephemeral present captured through capital or spectacle. Indeed, these issues that are raised in the Generation X novels are applicable to the authors' own sense of the weakening of their authority. In their writing, Spanish Generation X novelists come across as navigating uncertain ground. They deal with the divide between popular culture and "high" culture, and they are aware that that divide has been obfuscated by the demands of the market. They are also cognizant of the fact that they communicate through conventions of audiovisual media, which are often associated with, and dismissed as, mere entertainment. In these conditions Spanish Generation X novelists and their works are very much like their own subjects—they are individuals desirous of defining themselves in a context in which their agency is undermined by powerful forces outside of the self: the media and capital.

Notes

INTRODUCTION

1. The group is often referred to as Generación X after the characters of Douglas Coupland's novel of the same name, *Generation X* (1991). Coupland's novel was published in Spanish by Ediciones B in fall 1993. Spanish critics appear to prefer Generación Kronen in describing the same group following the 1994 publication of *Historias del Kronen* by representative author José Ángel Mañas. Carmen de Urioste prefers to call them, "Primera generación de la democracia española" (The first generation of democratic Spain) and as such points to the significant fact that the group is representative of a generation of Spanish people who grew up in democratic Spain and who did not experience the civil war nor the dictatorship following the civil war. For José María Izquierdo the denomination "narradores españoles novísimos" (most recent Spanish novelists) is preferable because of its neutrality. Unfortunately, it is so neutral that it does not assign a historical context to the group. In a recent publication, Ángel García Galiano has added the name "Generación Apolo" (2004, 56) to the list. With it he marks the impact of the advent of television in Spain on the formative years of his generation of writers. I classify the group of writers studied in this book as a "generation" because, in addition to the chronological link, they share some common experiences peculiar to their age and the times that have contributed to shaping their perception of the world and its expression in their works. All translations in this book are mine unless otherwise noted.

2. Javier Memba puts the number of published "young" writers in the 1990s at about sixty ("¿Qué se publica hoy en España? El boom de la novela joven," http:/www.elmundo.es/elmundolibro/2000/09/24/anticuario/969617385.html).

3. *Muertos o algo mejor* (Montesinos 1996). Hernando says she wrote this first novel inspired by "las preguntas que me hago sobre el mundo" (the questions that I ask myself about the world) She added that "[l]os protagonistas de la novela se hacen las mismas preguntas que yo, sobre el sentido de la vida y esas cosas. Quiero contar cómo somos los jóvenes de ahora, cómo vemos esa realidad que los adultos intentan ignorar" (the protagonists of the novel ask the same questions as I do about the meaning of life and so on. I want to tell a story about how young people are today, how we see that reality that adults try to ignore) (quoted in Xavier Moret, *El País*, culture section, March 12, 1996).

4. At the age of twenty-three Carmen Laforet published her first novel, *Nada*. It won the prestigious Premio Nadal in 1945 over the submission by César González Ruano, the already established and very well-known novelist and journalist who was also a Franco sympathizer.

5. Contrary to this vision, however, only the third of the first three publications by Lengua de Trapo, *Trece historias breves*, featured novelists such as Juan

154

Bonilla, José Ángel Mañas, and Daniel Múgica, who were just beginning to make their name as young writers. They first published a collection of crime fiction (*Malos tiempos*) by Juan Madrid who is a seasoned author in that genre and *Picatostes y otros textos*, by the first-time but not necessarily young writer Borja Delclaux, who also won the first Premio Lengua de Trapo. (Ángeles García, "Nace Lengua de Trapo, una editorial para nuevos autores," *El País*, culture section, December 14, 1995).

6. The following all appeared in the culture section of *El País* on the dates given: Pedro Sorela, April 23, 1993; Rosa Mora, January 6, 1995; Maite Río, April 26, 1997.

7. *La pistola de mi hermano* was originally published as *Caídos del cielo* [Fallen from heaven].

CHAPTER 1. CONSUMING AND COMMUNICATING

1. Film versions of three of the novels discussed in this book are as follows: *Historias del Kronen*, directed by Montxo Armendáriz, 1995; *La pistola de mi hermano*, directed by Ray Loriga, 1997; and *Las razones de mis amigos*, directed by Gerardo Herrero, 2000 (Adaptation of *La conquista del aire*).

2. Miguel Mora, "Gabriela Bustelo inventa un mundo futuro gobernado por mujeres," culture section, *El País*, July 16, 2001.

3. *El nido de Adán* [Adam's Rib] is the Spanish version of the original *Rebro Adama*, also known as *Adam's Rib* and *La côte d'Adán*, directed by Vyacheslav Krishtofovich, 1990. "Romer" refers to French film director Éric Rohmer.

4. *My Brother's Gun*, trans. Kristina Cordero (New York: St. Martin's Press, 1997). Unless otherwise noted all translations of excerpts of Ray Loriga's novel, *La pistola de mi hermano*, are from this source.

5. Translation modified.

6. Elvira Lindo, who also belongs to the Spanish Generation X group of writers, deals with the same theme in her novel *El otro barrio* [The other side]. In this novel the protagonist, who accidentally kills his friend one afternoon, is transformed by the flurry of newspaper articles and television and radio shows from a gentle, self-effacing young man into a depraved killer who supposedly commits murder because of his exposure to violent movies. To prove their theory, the creators of this easy media narrative claim that the "murderer" was watching the Oliver Stone film *Natural Born Killers* when he committed the crime. The truth is that he had planned to watch the movie with his friend; however, they ended up not watching it after all. Ironically this fiction created by the media leads to actions such as campaigns to remove the offending film from circulation.

7. My translation.

CHAPTER 2. URBAN FICTIONS/POPULAR FICTIONS

Versions of this chapter have been published in Spanish in *Confluencia* 20.1: 63–71 and *Revista Hispánica Moderna* 55.1 (2002): 204–10.

1. A good illustration of the significance of urban space in the determination of identity can be found in Luis Martín-Santos's novel *Tiempo de silencio* (1961) where he writes "un hombre es la imagen de una ciudad y una ciudad las vísceras puestas al revés de un hombre" (the human being is a reflection of the city and the city, the exposed entrails of the human being) and that "un hombre encuentra en su ciudad no sólo su determinación como persona y su razón de ser, sino también los impedimentos múltiples y los obstáculos invencibles que le impiden llegar a ser" (one finds in one's city not only one's affirmation as a person and one's *raison d'étre* but also the multiple impediments to one's being) (18).

2. Jean-Paul Sartre, *Nausea*, trans. Lloyd Alexander (New York: New Directions, 1964), 185.

3. Krutnik explains that the image of the morally upright male hero, which is subverted in the noir genre, is seen in the classic detective novels. These are characters who assert themselves as superior beings in the patriarchal context. That is, they are idealized as fine examples of male power, intelligence, aptitude for rationalization, and high moral standards.

4. "Castizo" means pure or authentic. It is applied to Madrid to describe neighborhoods and customs that its people consider to be truly and traditionally Madrilenian or icons of Madrilenian identity.

5. Françoise Peyrégne's study, in which she applies Augé's phenomenon of non-places to urban spaces and the disappearance of their symbolic value in Juan José Millás's novels, was instrumental in my application of this phenomenon to Bustelo's novel.

6. Augé, 107–8; his emphasis.

7. See Joan Ramon Resina's reasons for this close link between the urban setting and detective fiction. The main one rests on the notion of the modern city as "signos racionalmente interpretables, en oposición a los fundamentos míticos o rituales de la ciudad antigua . . . La lectura de los signos urbanos resulta posible en la medida en que la razón se impone a la oscuridad del enigma" (rationally interpretable signs, the opposite of the mythical and ritual basis of the old city . . . the reading of urban signs is possible insofar as reason is imposed on the obscurity of enigma) (1997, 146–47).

8. For Resina, anonymity in the urban setting is related to the origins of the detective genre (145). Basing his argument on a short story on anonymity in the city, "The Man of the Crowd," by Edgar Allan Poe, Resina writes that the detective is a product of the metropolis because he makes possible "la ocasión de ocultar . . . la individualidad" (the opportunity to hide . . . individuality) (146).

9. Gabriela Bustelo's most recent novel, *Planeta hembra* (Barcelona: RBA, 2001), continues to develop the idea of media of communication as voyeuristic tools that can be used to undermine democracy through the manipulation and control of the action of individuals.

10. Toni Dorca has identified the duplication of Vania's experience in the patient she meets at the mental institution as an example of the departure from unique events. He considers this to be characteristic of Spanish Generation X fiction (1997, 312–13).

CHAPTER 3. POWERLESS SUBJECTS

1. See *Ojáncano* (1999) where Gopegui writes of fiction that is contemporaneous with hers: "Sin duda la novela como medio ha ganado la partida, pervir-

tiendo de cualquier modo su origen y pasando a ser novela como medio para entretener (Undoubtedly fiction as a medium has won the game. Fiction has perverted its origins and has become a medium for entertainment) (87). She repeats the same observations in the prologue of *La conquista del aire* (10).

2. Ruiz de Elvira, *El País*, August 21, 1992.

3. Ibid.

4. "El 55% de los españoles rechaza la política económica aplicada por el gobierno," *El País*, August 21, 1992.

5. Xavier Moret, "Belén Gopegui plantea el miedo en el trabajo en su nuevo libro," *El País*, culture section, March 15, 2001.

6. The MATESA scandal shook and divided the Franco regime. Juan Vilá Reyes, president of MATESA allegedly obtained some ten billion pesetas in export credits illegally in collusion with some government officials. He was sentenced to several years in prison.

CHAPTER 4. INVENTING THE AUTHOR

1. Pepe Ortega and Paquito Ayala refer to two very significant Spanish men of letters, José Ortega y Gasset (1883–1955) and Francisco Ayala (1906–). The use of the diminutive of their names here denotes cheeky irony.

2. "La España que se ve desde Juan Goytisolo," *El País*, culture section, June 23, 2001.

3. Ibid.

4. Ibid.

5. Belausteguigoitia, *El País* culture section, September 29, 2000.

6. All omissions are the author's.

7. *The Adventures of Don Quixote*, trans. J. M. Cohen (New York: Penguin, 1950).

Bibliography

Acín, Ramón. 1996. "El comercio en la literatura: Un matrimonio difícil." *Ínsula* 589–90: 5–7

Afinoguénova, Eugenia. 2001. "Turistas y viajeros: Experiencia turística en la narrativa española del fin del siglo XX." *Revista de Estudios Hispánicos* 35: 281–92.

Agawu-Kakraba, Yaw. 2003. "Reading Modernism through Postmodernism: Antonio Orejudo Utrilla's *Fabulosas narraciones por historias.*" *Journal of Iberian and Latin American Studies* 9.2: 125–38.

Allinson, Mark. 2000. "The Construction of Youth in Spain in the 1980s and 1990s." In *Contemporary Spanish Cultural Studies*, ed. Barry Jordan and Rikki Morgan-Tamosunas, 265–73. New York: Oxford University Press.

Alonso, Santos. 2003. *La novela española en el fin de siglo: 1975–2001.* Madrid: Mare Nostrum.

Annesley, James. 1998. *Blank Fictions.* New York: St. Martin's Press.

Augé, Marc. 1995. *Non-Places: Introduction to an Anthropology of Supermodernity.* Trans. John Howe. London: Verso.

Baudrillard, Jean. 1998. *The Consumer Society: Myths and Structures.* Trans. George Ritzer. London: Sage Publications.

———. 1988. *Jean Baudrillard: Selected Writings.* Ed. Mark Poster. Stanford, CA: Stanford University Press.

Belausteguigoitia, Santiago. 2000. " 'Las personas no somos otra cosa que Literatura,' afirma Orejudo al presentar su novela *Ventajas de viajar en tren.*" *El País*, culture section, September 29.

Bradbury, Malcolm. 1991. "The Cities of Modernism." In *Modernism: A Guide to European Literature, 1890–1930*, ed. Malcolm Bradbury and James McFarlane, 96–104. London: Penguin Books.

Brand, Dana. 1990. "From the Flaneur to the Detective: Interpreting the City in Poe." In *Popular Fiction: Technology, Ideology, Production, Reading*, ed. Tony Bennett, 220–40. London: Routledge.

Bustamante, Enrique. 1995. "The Mass Media: A Problematic Modernization." In *Spanish Cultural Studies: An Introduction; The Struggle for Modernity*, ed. Helen Graham and Jo Labanyi. New York: Oxford University Press.

Bustelo, Gabriela. 1996. *Veo veo.* Barcelona: Anagrama.

———. 2001. *Planeta hembra.* Barcelona: RBA.

Casariego, Martín. 1992. *Algunas chicas son como todas.* Madrid: Plot Ediciones.

Castells, Manuel. 1996. *The Information Age: Economy, Society and Culture*, vol. 1, *The Rise of the Network Society*. Oxford: Blackwell.

———. 1997. *The Information Age: Economy, Society and Culture*, vol. 2, *The Power of Identity*. Oxford: Blackwell.

———. 1998. *The Information Age: Economy, Society and Culture*, vol. 3, *End of the Millennium*. Oxford: Blackwell.

Cawelti, John. 1977. "The Writer as a Celebrity: Some Aspects of American Literature as Popular Culture." *Studies in American Fiction* 5.1: 161–74.

Caws, Mary Ann. 1991. Introduction, in *City Images: Perspectives from Literature, Philosophy and Film*, ed. Mary Ann Caws, 1–11. New York: Gordon and Breach.

Cela, Camilo José. 1998. *La colmena*. Madrid: Alianza.

Cercas, Javier. 2001. "Sobre los incovenientes de escribir en libertad." http://www.literaturas.com/cercas.htm.

Cervantes Saavedra, Miguel de. 1992. *Don Quijote de la Mancha*. Ed. Martín de Riquer. Barcelona: Editorial Juventud. Trans. J. M. Cohen as *The Adventures of Don Quixote*. New York: Penguin, 1950.

Chandler, Raymond. 1972. *Trouble is My Business*. New York: Ballantine.

Clark, T. J. 1985. *The Painting of Modern Life*. London: Thames and Hudson.

Cone, Annabelle. 1996. "Misplaced Desire: The Female Urban Experience in Colette and Rohmer." *Literature Film Quarterly* 24.4: 423–31.

Coupland, Douglas. 1991. *Generation X: Tales for an Accelerated Culture*. New York: St. Martin's Press.

———. *Microserfs*. 1995. New York: HaperCollins.

Curtis, Margarita O'Byrne. 1996. "Madrid o la locura del texto urbano: La representación de la ciudad en la narrativa galdosiana." In *Studies in Honor of Gilberto Paolini*, ed. Mercedes Vidal Tibbitts and Claire J. Paolini, 195–206. Newark: Cuesta.

The Dark Corner. 1946. Directed by Henry Hathaway. Twentieth Century Fox.

Davenport, Gary. 1988. "Urban Fiction Today." *Sewanee Review* 96.4:695–702.

Dawson, Paul. 1997. "Grunge Lit: Marketing Generation X." *Meanjin:* 119–25

Dear, Michael J. 2000. *The Postmodern Urban Condition*. Oxford: Blackwell, 2000.

De Répide, Pedro. 1995. *Las calles de Madrid*. Madrid: Ediciones la librería.

Detour. 1945. Directed by Edgar G. Ulmer.

Díaz, José Simón. 1993. *Guía literaria de Madrid: De murallas adentro*. Vol. 1. Madrid: Ediciones la librería.

———. *Guía literaria de Madrid: Arrabales y Barrios Bajos*. Vol 2. Madrid: Ediciones la librería.

Doane, Mary Anne. 1991. *Femmes Fatales: Feminism, Film Theory Psychoanalysis*. New York: Routledge.

Dorca, Toni. 1997. "Joven narrativa en la España de los noventa: La generación X." *Revista de Estudios Hispánicos* 31.2:309–24.

Double Indemnity. 1994. Directed by Billy Wilder. Paramount.

Dunn, Robert G. 1998. *Identity Crises: A Social Critique of Postmodernity*. Minneapolis: University of Minnesota Press.

Echevarría, Ignacio. 2003. "El tinglado de los premios." *El País*, Babelia, May 10, 14.

Edenbaum, Robert. 1968. "The Poetics of the Private Eye: The Novels of Dashiell Hammett." In *Tough Guy Writers of the Thirties*, ed. David Madden, 80–103. Carbondale: University of Illinois Press.

Ellis, Bret Easton. 1991. *American Psycho*. New York: Vintage.

Etxebarria, Lucía. 1998. *Beatriz y los cuerpos celestes*. Barcelona: Destino.

Fajardo, José Manuel. 2000. *La huella de unas palabras: Antología de Antonio Muñoz Molina*. Madrid: Espasa Calpe.

Featherstone, Mike, ed. 1990. *Global Culture: Nationalism, Globalization and Modernity*. London: Sage Publications.

Freire, Espido. 1999. *Melocotones helados*. Barcelona: Planeta.

Fowler, Alastair. 1979. "Genre and Literary Canon." *New Literary History* 11:97–119.

Fuguet, Alberto, and Sergio Gómez. 1996. *McOndo*. Barcelona: Grijalbo-Mondadori.

García, Ángeles. 1995. "Nace Lengua de Trapo, una editorial para nuevos autores." *El País*, culture section, December 14.

García Galiano, Ángel. 2004. "Desarraigo, adolescencia y extravagancia: Esbozo de poética en la narrativa de mi generación." In *En cuarentena: Nuevos narradores y críticos a principios del siglo XXI*, ed. Antonio Orejudo, 39–64. Murcia: Universidad de Murcia.

García Luis. "Antonio Orejudo." http:/www.literaturas.com/antoniorejudo.htm.

García Serrano, Yolanda, and Verónica Fernández. 2001. *De qué va eso del amor*. Barcelona: Destino.

Gavira Martín, José, and Carmen Gavira Golpe. 1999. *Madrid: Centro y periferia*. Madrid: Biblioteca Nueva.

Gea Ortigas, María Isabel. 1999. *Los nombres de las calles de Madrid*. 3rd edition. Madrid: Ediciones de la librería.

Gelfant, Blanche Houseman. 1954. *The American City Novel*. Norman: University of Oklahoma Press.

Gil Casado, Pablo. 1968. *La novela social española (1942–1968)*. Barcelona: Seix Barral.

Gopegui, Belén. 1998. *La conquista del aire*. Barcelona: Anagrama.

———. 1999. "Contribución acerca del sentido de *La conquista del aire*." *Ojáncano* 16:86–89.

———. 2000. *Lo real*. Barcelona: Anagrama.

———. 2001a. "Academia." *El País*, September 15.

———. 2001b. "Ser infierno." *Revista Cervantes* [Instituto Cervantes de Milan] 0:23–31.

Goytisolo, Juan. 2001. "Vamos a menos." *El País*, opinion section, January 10.

Graham, Helen, and Antonio Sánchez. 1995. "The Politics of 1992." In *Spanish*

Cultural Studies: An Introduction, The Struggle for Modernity, ed. Helen Graham and Jo Labanyi, 406–18. New York: Oxford University Press.

Grasa, Ismael. 1994. *De Madrid al cielo*. Barcelona: Anagrama.

Gullón, Germán. 1996. "Cómo se lee una novela de la última generación (apartado x)." *Ínsula* 589–90:31–33.

———. 1997. "La conflictiva recepción de la novela joven: *Soy un escritor frustrado*, de José Ángel Mañas." *Ínsula* 605:13–15.

———. 2004a. *Los mercaderes en el templo de la literatura*. Madrid: Caballo de Troya.

———. 2004b. "La novela en España: 2004; Un espacio para el encuentro." *Ínsula* 668:2–4.

Gutiérrez Resa, Antonio. 2003. *Sociología de valores en la novela contemporánea española/(La generación X)*. Madrid: Fundación Santa María.

Hall, Peter. 1998. *Cities in Civilization: Culture, Innovation, and Urban Order*. London: Phoenix Giant.

Heriz, Enrique de. 1994. *El día menos pensado*. Barcelona: Ediciones B.

Herzberger, David. 1998. "Writing Without a Grain: Identity Formation in Three Works by Muñoz Molina." *Arizona Journal of Hispanic Cultural Studies* 2:23–40.

Holloway, Vance, R. 1999. *El posmodernismo y otras tendencias de la novela española (1967–1995)*. Madrid: Editorial Fundamentos.

Howe, Irving. 1971. "The City in Literature." *Commentary* 51:61–68.

In a Lonely Place. 1950. Directed by Nicholas Ray. Columbia.

Inglis, Fred. 1988. *Popular Culture and Political Power*. New York: St. Martin's Press.

Izquierdo, José María. 2001. "Narradores españoles novísimos de los años noventa." *Revista de Estudios Hispánicos* 35:293–308.

Jameson, Fredric. 1991. *Postmodernism or, the Cultural Logic of Late Capitalism*. Durham, NC: Duke University Press.

Jiménez Sánchez, Fernando. 1995. *Detrás del escándalo político: Opinión pública, dinero y poder en la España del siglo XX*. Barcelona: Tusquets.

Juliá, Santos. 1999. *Un siglo de España: Política y Sociedad*. Madrid: Marcial Pons.

Juliá, Santos, David Ringrose, and Cristina Segura. 1998. *Madrid: Historia de una capital*. Madrid: Alianza Editorial.

Kaplan, E. Anne, ed. 1998. *Women in Film Noir*. Rev. ed. London: British Film Institute.

Kawin, Bruce F. 1982. *The Mind of the Novel: Reflexive Fiction and the Ineffable*. Princeton: Princeton University Press.

Kerr, Paul. 1990. "Out of What Past? Notes on the B *Film Noir*. In *Popular Fiction: Technology, Ideology, Production, Reading*, ed. Tony Bennett, 375–94. London: Routledge.

Krutnik, Frank. 1991. *In a Lonely Street: Film Noir, Genre, Masculinity*. London: Routledge.

Labanyi, Jo. 1995a. "Postmodernism and the Problem of Cultural Identity." In

Spanish Cultural Studies: An Introduction, ed. Helen Graham and Jo Labanyi, 396–406. New York: Oxford University Press.

———. 1995b. "Literary Experiment and Cultural Cannibalization." In *Spanish Cultural Studies: An Introduction*, ed. Helen Graham and Jo Labanyi, 295–99. New York: Oxford University Press.

Lacarta, Manuel. 1986. *Madrid y sus literaturas*. Madrid: El Avapiés.

Lasch, Christopher. 1984. *The Minimal Self: Psychic Survival in Troubled Times*. London: W. W. Norton.

Lash, Scott. 1990. *Sociology of Postmodernism*. London: Routledge.

Lasn, Kalle. 2000. "Cultural Jamming." In *The Consumer Society Reader*, ed. Juliet B. Schor and Douglas B. Holt, 415–32. New York: New York Press.

Lehan, Richard. 1986. "Urban Signs and Urban Literature: Literary Form and Historical Process." *New Literary History* 18.1:99–113.

Lindo, Elvira. 1999. *El otro barrio*. Madrid: Santillana.

Lodge, David. 2002. "Dickens Our Contemporary." *Atlantic Online*, May.

Loriga, Ray. 1995. *La pistola de mi hermano* (*Caídos del cielo*). Barcelona: Plaza y Janés. Trans. Kristina Cordero as *My Brother's Gun*. New York: St. Martin's Press, 1997.

———. Director. 1997. *La pistola de mi hermano*. Film adaptation.

Lyon, David. 1999. *Postmodernity*. 2nd ed. Minneapolis: University of Minnesota Press.

Machnikowski, Ryszard M. 2000. "The Ideology of Globalization, the Globalization of the Ideology." In *Transatlantic Studies*, ed. Will Kaufman and Heidi Slettedahl, 87–96, Lanham, MD: University Press of America.

Maestre, Pedro. 1999. *Matando dinosaurios con tirachinas*. Barcelona: Ediciones Destino.

The Maltese Falcon. 1941. Directed by John Huston. Warner Bros.

Mañas, José Ángel. 1994. *Historias del Kronen*. Barcelona: Destino.

———. 1996. *Soy un escritor frustrado*. Madrid: Espasa-Calpe.

Mañas, José Ángel, and Montxo Armendáriz, directors. 1995. *Historias del Kronen*. Film Adaptation.

Marías, Fernando. 2001. *El niño de los coroneles*. Barcelona: Destino.

Martín-Santos, Luis. 1999. *Tiempo de silencio*. Barcelona: Seix Barral.

Maurell, Pilar. 1998. " 'No acepto las reglas del juego tipo dinero fácil, lectura fácil': Belén Gopegui publica su tercera novela, *La conquista del aire*, la historia final de una utopía ya gastada." *El Mundo*, January 31.

Maxfield, James F. 1996. *The Fatal Woman: Sources of Male Anxiety in American Film Noir, 1941–1991*. London: Associated University Presses.

Maxwell, Richard. 1995. *The Spectacle of Democracy: Spanish Television, Nationalism, and Political Transition*. Minneapolis: University of Minnesota Press.

Memba, Javier. 2000. "¿Qué se publica hoy en España?: El boom de la novela joven." http://www.elmundo.es/elmundolibro/2000/09/24/anticuario/969617385.html

Montero Alonso, José et al. 1990, *Diccionario General de Madrid*. Madrid: Méndez y Molina.

Montetes Mairal, Noemí. 1999. *Qué he hecho yo para publicar esto: XX escritores jóvenes para el siglo XXI*. Barcelona: DVD ediciones.

Mora, Miguel. 2002. "Dudas y certezas de una generación dispersa y sin bar." *El País*, culture section, November 12.

Mora, Rosa 1995. "La literatura supeditada a las leyes del mercado." *El País*, culture section, January 6.

Moret, Xavier. 2001. "Belén Gopegui plantea el miedo en el trabajo en su nuevo libro." *El Pais*, culture section, March 15.

———. 1996. "Violeta Hernando publica a los 14, años una novela de sexo, droga y 'rock and roll.'" *El País*, culture section March 12.

Moreiras Menor, Cristina. 2000. "Spectacle, Trauma and Violence in Contemporary Spain." In *Contemporary Spanish Cultural Studies*, ed. Barry Jordan and Rikki Morgan-Tamosunas, 134–42. London: Arnold.

Morgan, Tony. 2000. "1992: Memories and Modernities." In *Contemporary Spanish Cultural Studies*, ed. Barry Jordan and Rikki Morgan-Tamosunas, 58–67. New York: Arnold.

Muñoz Molina, Antonio. 1989. *Beltenebros*. Barcelona: Plaza y Janés.

Naremore, James. 1998. *More Than Night: Film Noir in Its Contexts*. Berkeley: University of California Press.

Navajas, Gonzalo. 1996. *Más allá de la posmodernidad: Estética de la nueva novela y cine españoles*. Barcelona: EUB.

———. 2002. *La narrativa española en la era global: Imagen, comunicación, ficción*. Barcelona: EUB.

———. 2004. "La novela española de la pos-nación." *Ínsula* 688:13–8.

Navarro, Vicenç. 2002. *Bienestar insuficiente, democracia incompleta: De lo que no se habla en nuestro país*. Barcelona: Anagrama.

Olalquiaga, Celeste. 1992. Megalopolis: Contemporary Cultural Sensibilities. Minneapolis: University of Minnesota Press.

Orejudo Utrilla, Antonio. 2000. *Ventajas de viajar en tren*. Madrid: Santillana.

———. 2001a. *Fabulosas narraciones por historias*. Madrid: Suma de letras.

———. 2001b. "Buscando el baúl de los recuerdos: Novela, sociedad, ideología y compromiso." *Revista electrónica de estudios filológicos 2:1–8. www.um.es/tonosdigital/znum2/estudios/OrejudoTonos2.htm*.

———. *2004. "La literatura del boom* (demográfico) español. *Ínsula* 688: 7–8.

Palacios Bañuelos, Luis. 2001. *Reflexiones sobre la España de fin de siglo*. Madrid: Editorial Centro de Estudios Ramón Areces.

Peyrègne, Françoise. 1997. "Espacio urbano, espacio íntimo en la novela de Juan José Millás. In *"Historia, Espacio e imaginario*, ed. Jacqueline Covo and Maria Ghazali, 71–77. Villeneuve d'Ascq: Septentrion.

Pike, Burton. 1981. *The Image of the City in Modern Literature*. Princeton: Princeton University Press.

Porfirio, Robert G. 1996. "No Way Out: Existential Motifs in the Film Noir." In *Perspectives on "Film Noir,"* 115–28. Toronto: Prentice Hall.

The Postman Always Rings Twice. 1946. Directed by Tay Garnet. Metro-Goldwyn-Mayer.

Postman, Neil. 1985. *Amusing Ourselves to Death: Public Discourse in the Age of Show Business.* New York: Viking.

Prada, Juan Manuel de. 1997. *La tempestad.* Barcelona: Planeta.

Preston, Paul. 1992. "Materialism and 'serie negra.'" In *Leeds Papers on Thrillers in the Transition: "Novela negra" and Political Change in Spain,* ed. Rob Rix, 9–16. Leeds: Trinity and All Saints.

Resina, Joan Ramon. 1997. *El cadáver en la cocina: La novela criminal en la cultura del desencanto.* Barcelona: Anthropos.

Richardson, Bill. 2001. *Spanish Studies: An Introduction.* London: Arnold.

Río, Maite. 1997. "La literatura se volvió mercado pero hay que tener fe en las letras." *El País,* culture section, April 26.

Rivera de la Cruz, Marta. "Belén Gopegui." http://www.ucm.es/info/especulo/ numero7/gopegui.htm.

Rodríguez Marcos, Javier. "Ray Loriga." *El País,* Babelia, January 31, 2–3.

Romero Salvadó, Francisco J. 1999. *Twentieth-Century Spain: Politics and Society in Spain, 1898–1998.* New York: St. Martin's Press.

Ruiz de Elvira, Malen. 1992. "Todo preparado para el lanzamiento del satélite 'Hispasat,' tercer gran acontecimiento del 92." *El País,* society section, August 21.

Santos, Care. 2004. "La voz del yo en la novela última: Una teoría en busca de cómplice." *Ínsula* 688:8–11.

Sanz Villanueva, Santos. 1998. "Poderoso caballero: Gopegui publica su novela más ambiciosa y completa." *El Mundo,* February 21.

Sartre, Jean-Paul. 1966. *La nausée.* Paris: Gallimard. Trans. Lloyd Alexander as *Nausea.* New York: New Directions, 1964.

Sieburth, Stephanie. 1994. *Inventing High and Low: Literature, Mass Culture, and Uneven Modernity in Spain.* Durham, NC: Duke University Press.

Silva, Lorenzo. 2000. *El alquimista impaciente.* Barcelona: Destino.

Sorela, Pedro. 1993. "El mercado impone una literatura ligera." *El País,* Culture section, April 23.

Spires, Robert C. 1996. *Post-Totalitarian Spanish Fiction.* Columbia: University of Missouri Press.

Stables, Kate. 1998. "The Postmodern Always Rings Twice: Constructing the Femme Fatale in '90s Cinema." In *Women in Film Noir,* ed. E. Ann Kaplan. London: British Film Institute.

Telotte, J. P. 1989. *Voices in the Dark: The Narrative Patterns in Film Noir.* Urbana: University of Illinois Press.

Touraine, Alain. 1971. *The Post-Industrial Society; Tomorrow's Social History: Classes, Conflicts, and Culture in the Programmed Society.* Trans. Leonard F. X. Mayhew. New York: Random House.

———. 1988. *Return of the Actor: Social Theory in Postindustrial Society.* Trans. Myrna Godzich. Minneapolis: University of Minnesota Press.

———. 1995. *Critique of Modernity.* Trans. David Macey. Oxford: Blackwell.

———. 1997. *What is Democracy?* Trans. David Macey. Boulder: Westview Press.

———. 1998. "Social Transformations of the Twentieth Century." *International Social Science Journal* 50.156:165–71.

The Truman Show. 1998. Directed by Peter Weir. Starring Jim Carrey, Laura Linney, Noah Emmerich, Natascha McElhone, Holland Taylor, and Ed Harris. Paramount Pictures.

Tuska, Jon. 1984. *Dark Cinema: American Film Noir in Cultural Perspective*. Westport, CT: Greenwood.

Umbral Francisco. 2001. "Los placeres y los días: Belén Gopegui." *El Mundo* March 29.

Urioste, Carmen de. 1997. "La narrativa española de los noventa: ¿Existe una 'generación X'?" *Letras Peninsulares* 10.3:455–76.

Vázquez Montalbán, Manuel. 1998. *La literatura en la construcción de la ciudad democrática*. Barcelona: Grijalbo Mondadori.

Wallace, David Foster. 1997. *A Supposedly Fun Thing I'll Never Do Again: Essays and Arguments*. Boston: Little, Brown.

Waugh, Patricia. 1984. *Metafiction: The Theory and Practice of Self-Conscious Fiction*. London: Methuen.

Index

166